FRED T. MERCADANTE

SENIOR HIGH
MINISTRY THAT
works!

A PARISH-BASED
INITIATION
MODEL

TWENTY
THIRD 23rd
PUBLICATIONS

Special thanks goes to
Sylvia McGeary, Maris Barrett, and Kurt Kilanowski
for their contributions, knowledge, and support.

Cover photo: ©iStockphoto.com/Aldo Murillo

Twenty-Third Publications
A Division of Bayard
One Montauk Avenue, Suite 200
New London, CT 06320
(860) 437-3012 or (800) 321-0411
www.23rdpublications.com

ISBN 978-1-58595-704-0
Library of Congress Catalog Card Number: 2008925304
Printed in the U.S.A.

Contents

Dear pastors, pastoral associates, professional youth and young adult ministers, diocesan coordinators, DREs, volunteer ministers, and (dare I say) bishops:

This book will help you!

Especially if....

- You would love to see more young people and their families come to Mass.

- You would love to be confident that the young people and their families who do come to Mass know why they are there.

- You want to tap into the energy of young people.

- You want to see teenagers remain active in the life of the parish after confirmation.

- You want to be a coordinator of service opportunities rather than a probation officer.

- You want youth ministry to give you life rather than suck it out of you.

- You want to be able to use all your gifts.

- You believe that faith is caught, not taught.

- You believe that children and youth are just as much a part of the Church as any adult.

- You believe that the word "intergenerational" can be a reality rather than a nice thought.

- You believe in parish.

- You live in the image and likeness of a creative God.

- You want a strong youth ministry in your parish that is not in competition with other parish ministries.

- You believe that there is a huge developmental difference between freshmen and seniors that demands age-appropriate catechesis.

- You are most concerned that young people are developing into an adult faith.

So how does a parish youth minister get to the point of authoring a strategy book for youth ministry? If someone were to tell me fourteen years ago that I would be writing a book on youth ministry, not only would I not have believed it, but I probably would have verbally crucified that person. I don't know why it angered me so back then when people would suggest that I would make a great youth minister someday. Maybe it was because I didn't want women to think that I was unavailable (even though youth ministers do not take a vow of celibacy), but whatever the case I did not want to work for the Church. Volunteering was the extent to which my "still forming self" would venture.

But then something happened that I did not expect: two years after graduating from college, I still could not find a job with a career path. So when Fr. Ron Amandolare of St. Patrick Church in Chatham, New Jersey (my home parish) asked me if I would consider becoming the parish's next youth ministry coordinator, I finally thought to myself, "Hey, you know, I bet I would make a great youth minister!" So I agreed to do the job for a year and then decide if I liked it.

Well, here we are fourteen years later. I have a Masters degree in pastoral ministry with a specialization in adolescence. I have been to numerous conferences and workshops. I have written two retreat processes and have been hired to consult with many other parishes. My favorite book of all time is *Doing the Truth in Love* by Fr. Michael Himes (mind you, it's my favorite book, not just my favorite work-related book). I'd say that I have changed quite a bit in the last fourteen years!

Now I find myself working and ministering within a Church where my peers have either written us off or have come back to get their babies baptized. I see so many of my peers still where I was fourteen years ago. My faith stopped forming once I went away to college (which is actually better than most, whose faith stopped forming after confirmation). As of today, my number one concern as a youth minister is to help young people develop into an adult faith that will not stop forming just because formal religious education stops.

Introduction

Imagine this scene: a mid-sized suburban parish calls a meeting for all high school freshmen and their parents. It is the first meeting of the year, and it serves as an introduction to senior high youth ministry and consequently, confirmation preparation.

The youth minister who is directing the meeting begins with an ice breaker and opening prayer. Then, before she says anything of substance, a dialogue is opened.

Youth Minister So, freshmen, why are you here? (*The question is followed by silence*) Come on people, why are you here? You can be honest. Anyone? (*The young people look at their friends with that familiar adolescent smirk and then look at their parents to try to sense if it is alright to speak freely. Still, no one volunteers.*) You, why are you here?

Young Boy (*Answers with a question*) To learn about God and stuff?

Youth Minister Alright, how about you?

Shy Young Girl (*Timidly*) I don't know, same as what he said I guess.

Youth Minister To learn about God and stuff! Anyone else? What about you?

Brave Young Boy Because my mom made me come. (*Laughter*)

Youth Minister Honesty! I like it! Couple more..., you there. (*Hands are going up now*)

Confident Boy To get confirmed.

Youth Minister Makes sense. One more. How about you?

Logical Girl Because you told us to come.

Youth Minister I did? When?

Logical Girl You sent us a letter and told us to come.

Youth Minister Oh, the letter. Well, if you go home and read that letter again, you just might see that it was more of an invitation than anything else, but hey, if that's what you got out of the letter, far be it from me to criticize. Now, how about the parents here? Why are you here? And you can't say "To learn about God and stuff," because that's already been taken.

Parent One To find out what my daughter has to do in order to be confirmed.

Youth Minister Okay. I'm sure we'll cover that.

Parent Two I want my son to have what I had.

Youth Minister If you don't mind me asking, what did you have that you want your son to have?

Parent Two Well, when I was his age, I went to Mass every week with my family and I learned about the saints and how to say the different prayers and about the Ten Commandments and things like that. I want him to learn about our religion and be proud of it.

Youth Minister Thank you. Anyone else?

Parent Three I guess then that I want my daughter to have what I didn't have. Because I went to Mass every week with my parents too, but I didn't really learn anything. I want my daughter to learn something.

Youth Minister Alright. Someone has a hand up in the back.

Parent Four Yeah, I wasn't going to raise my hand but you know, I hated going to church when I was a teenager. It was boring and I really didn't care about what they were trying to teach me. And I just really want my daughter to know that it's okay to have fun at church. Don't get me wrong. I want her to learn about "God and stuff" too, but in a fun and interesting way.

Youth Minister Well then, hopefully what I introduce to you tonight will address all of these wants.

Anyone who works in parish youth ministry where the sacrament of confirmation is celebrated at a junior high school or senior high school level will be very familiar with this type of dialogue. Every answer to the question, "Why are you here?" by both the youth and their parents is pretty much what we in Church leadership should expect. Their answers reflect an American Church in transition and a Church that is still forming an identity since Vatican II.

"WHY ARE YOU HERE?"

"To learn about God and stuff?" The young boy answers with a question. He thinks that the youth minister is looking for a specific answer. He is programmed by an academic society. He spends most of his time in a classroom and therefore assumes that the Church is a classroom as well. Who can blame him? The Church has been a classroom in many ways for many decades. In the pages to come, this book will put forth an attitude toward youth ministry that breaks through the walls of the classroom and moves into all facets of life. "Attitude" is the key word because much of what is written here is not really new strategy. It's a combination of strategies that frees us from the shackles of a "youth program" and reclaims an initiatory attitude toward senior high youth ministry.

"Because my mom made me come." Let's face it, in an ideal world, freshmen in high school would willingly come to church without pressure from their parents. But realistically, even the best parents in the world will have teenagers who need to be prodded to do things simply because of the nature of adolescence. I always tell parents of freshmen that if they have to make their kids get involved in youth ministry at first, that just may be a necessary evil. But if they are still making their teen participate after a year or so, then we have to talk. A good youth ministry will help foster the ongoing conversion process that began in childhood and continues on through adolescence and adulthood. A good youth ministry will eventually see young people begin to voluntarily participate when their conversion process shifts from a "faith given" to a "faith owned." The suggestions offered in this book will help parishes establish this "good youth ministry" for which we are all striving.

"To get confirmed." In my opinion, one of the worst things that we in Church leadership have done is to present our sacraments (especially the sacraments of initiation) as things we obtain or "get." Too often in our Church, confirmation is perceived as something you get if you jump through the right hoops and complete all the requirements. Many of us in parish leadership complain that too many young people see confirmation as an end or a graduation from the parish. Even as we insist that confirmation is a beginning, faith formation and parish participation can easily come to an end with confirmation. With this in mind, we the Church can ask ourselves: "Why do so many Catholics view confirmation as an end?" In her book *Fashion Me a People*, Maria Harris deals with this topic in a more broad sense by taking a look at our language:

My own educational work is a search to find new ways of speaking about this, since the language we use to describe our work has enormous power, either to support or to undermine what we are attempting to do. (Harris, pp. 39-40)

According to Harris, who takes an in-depth look at the language we use in religious education, by understanding education as much more than "schooling," we can begin to breakdown the misconception that education is only for the young. In a similar fashion, this book will examine how we speak and think about youth ministry (and consequently the sacrament of confirmation) with an eye toward how our language affects (positively and negatively) what we are trying to accomplish (i.e. receive confirmation vs. celebrate confirmation).

"Because you told us to come." Even though a 2002 *Special Report on Young Adult Catholics* by the Center for Applied Research in the Apostolate (CARA, p. 5) suggests that in general younger generations of American Catholics are moving away from viewing the Church as an authority, there are still elements of a "tell me what to do and what not to do" attitude, even among our young people. Young people today are presented with far more options than even the youth from ten years ago. It has reached a point in our society that now our young people cannot deal with all of the choices. Perhaps as a defense mechanism, some adolescents will actually seek out less freedom (quite different from the youth of previous generations). There is no doubt that many youth are not getting parameters at home (even from the most conservative households) and therefore may want someone in authority to tell them what to do. "I am here because you, a person of authority, told me I had to come, and I'm just following orders." This is a unique problem that we are facing. How do we not revert back to a pre-Vatican II attitude of letting Church authority think for us when our society offers far too many choices for one person to handle? Answer: read on!

"To find out what my daughter has to do in order to be confirmed." Does this sound familiar? It should, because it goes back even to the time of Jesus. Recall Matthew 19:16–30, Mark 10:17–31, and Luke 18:18–30: "Master, what do I have to do in order to have eternal life?" Jesus responds, "Obey the commandments." Response: "I have done this; what else do I have to do?" Jesus drops a bomb: "If you want to be perfect, sell all your belongings and follow me." The man goes away very sad because he cannot bring himself to do what Jesus suggests. Imagine if the youth minister addressed the parent's concern by responding: "In order to be confirmed, your teenage daughter must part with all selfishness. She must choose a lifestyle that is one of loving service to others. Her attitude must be the same as Jesus', the humble servant. Then and only then will she be able to confirm her baptism." Of course, answering the concern in that fashion would not be very pastoral and would probably come off as harsh; however, there are some questions here to consider.

Is it right for a parish to set minimum requirements that must be completed in order for one to be confirmed and/or should a certain level of conversion be reached as the criteria? Do parishes who prepare for confirmation at a high school level put too much emphasis on "the confirmation program" and not enough on total youth ministry? How much difference (if any) should there be between a senior high youth ministry in a diocese where the young people are confirmed before they reach high school and a diocese that confirms during the high school years? Do we, like Jesus, allow some people to walk away very sad when we suggest that there is more to Christian initiation than the "fulfillment of minimum requirements"? The teenage daughter of the parent may not have the "total conversion" that Jesus asks of the rich man, but she *can* be part of an ongoing conversion process fostered by a youth ministry within her

parish that will accept her no matter what. Keep in mind that we do not know what eventually happens to the rich man in the gospels. Perhaps years later he completely gives himself over to Jesus. This book will help you implement the kind of youth ministry that meets people where they are and allows them to journey at their own pace.

"I want my son to have what I had." This parent is going to have the hardest time accepting an "experience leads to learning" approach to youth ministry. As stated in *The Challenge of Adolescent Catechesis: Maturing in Faith*, "Adolescent catechesis is clearly in a state of transition, reflecting both the cultural and ecclesial shifts of the past two decades" (#3). The way this parent received religious instruction is notably different than the way her child will be formed. Today the Church is stressing experience just as much as indoctrination in respect to catechesis within youth ministry: "Experiential learning…gives rise to concerns and questions, hopes and anxieties, reflections and judgments, which increase one's desire to penetrate more deeply into life's meaning" (*Sharing the Light of Faith: National Catechetical Directory for Catholics of the United States*, 176d). The directory calls for ongoing faith experiences, which leads to ongoing faith formation. We the Church have recognized that it is the experience of God as lived out through the community that allows us to appreciate and internalize the facts of the faith and our prayer traditions. Experiential learning is at the heart of this book's suggested strategy for youth ministry catechesis.

"I want my daughter to have what I didn't have." This parent experienced the opposite end of the pendulum when the Church was stressing that "Jesus loves you," but was not making any real connection between the love of Jesus and our Catholic tradition. This parent feels "ripped off" because no one ever connected him to the reality that the basics of our faith can come alive! He wants more for his daughter. Young people today learn best through experience. This is undeniable. But experience must always lead to learning; otherwise, we might as well not have had the experience in the first place.

For example, I have seen parishes coordinate some great weekend retreat experiences for their youth. The Spirit of Jesus is alive and the love is so thick that it permeates the room. But when the experience is over and there is no ongoing follow-up (connected to our faith and tradition), the retreat becomes a one-shot deal, a one-time conversion experience, and in the long run, it doesn't make much of a difference in one's faith formation. The challenge explored in this book is not only to foster these Jesus experiences, but to unpack them so as to recognize how Scripture and tradition are and always have been intertwined with the "God experience."

"I want my daughter to know that it's okay to have fun at Church." In youth ministry, there is a balancing act that occurs between having fun and instilling a sense of sacredness. For example, I learned a valuable lesson early on as a young youth minister at a small group liturgy preparation meeting when I allowed some of the young people to wear hats, chew gum, lean on the altar, etc. in the church building. I was overly concerned that they were too uptight in the church. It took a colleague to point out that "comfortable" does not always mean "casual." Then, in another situation later on in my career, I unconsciously was so obsessed with sacredness while conducting a church tour that everything seemed to be "really serious" according to the youth who participated. I remember thinking to myself, "It's no wonder many youth have a difficult time imagining a laughing Jesus!" Moral of these stories: If we who coordinate youth ministry provide structure, instill a sense of the sacred, empower leadership, and grant free time, we will find that youth will be enriched in everything that we do. Everything is sacred, and a respect for people, places, and things will come naturally to our young people as long as our relationship with them is natural and as long as the education and discipline that we pass on is authentic and sincere.

If there is one thing I have learned, it is that youth ministry is a lot like the mystery of God: there is always more to experience and learn. This book will help you implement a parish youth ministry that works, but it leaves much room for you to make it work even better. So, let's get going.

SECTION ONE

A GOOD VISION AND A GOOD STRATEGY

A Good Vision
for Youth Ministry

The U.S. bishops spell out for us their vision of Catholic youth ministry through their document *Renewing the Vision*. In a sense, they are saying to all parishes, Catholic schools, and diocesan youth ministry offices that this is our common understanding of youth ministry, and we are all called to implement strategies that will make this vision a reality. It is our starting point.

Although the document never formally describes parish-based youth ministry, in the spirit of *Renewing the Vision*, we could describe in this way:

> Ongoing faith formation through which adolescents and their families live out their baptismal call within the life of their parish community.

According to the document, there are three main goals for youth ministry:

1. To empower young people to live as disciples of Jesus Christ in our world today.

2. To draw young people to responsible participation in the life, mission, and work of the Catholic faith community.

3. To foster the total personal and spiritual growth of each young person.

Finally, according to the document, there are eight components of comprehensive youth ministry:

Evangelization: Awakening others to the Good News of Jesus within every human situation and seeking to transform individuals and society by *being* the Good News. Answering the call of Jesus to "go and make disciples."

Community Life: Creating an atmosphere in your parish that is welcoming, comfortable, safe, and predictable—one in which all teens know that their presence is welcomed, their energy is appreciated, and their contributions are valued.

Leadership Development: Calling forth, affirming, empowering, and training adults and young people to use their diverse gifts, talents, and abilities.

Catechesis: Echoing the Word of God and passing on the Catholic tradition (as a way of expressing the Christian faith) to others so that they can grow and mature in *their* faith.

Prayer and Worship: Honoring, praising, and

communicating with God. Offering God the gift of ourselves through the Mass, the sacraments, prayers, and prayer services.

Justice and Service: The call to work for justice; to serve those in need; to pursue peace; and to defend the life, dignity, and rights of all our sisters and brothers.

Pastoral Care: The call to be a compassionate presence in imitation of Jesus' care of all people, especially those who are hurting and in need.

Advocacy: Engaging the Church to examine its priorities and practices to determine how well young people are integrated into the life, mission, and work of the Catholic community, and empowering young people and their families to speak for those who cannot speak.

The document clearly points out that it is a vision and a framework, not a model. It does not suggest how to do youth ministry, rather it simply spells out what it is.

When my home parish first began developing a new model of youth ministry that would best implement *Renewing the Vision*, I sat with the likes of John Roberto and Mike Moseley to pick their brains (two "giants" in the field of Catholic youth ministry in my estimation). One thing Mike Moseley said during our meeting is worth mentioning here: "As long as you stick with the eight components, you can't go wrong."

If a youth ministry can offer young people and their families an opportunity to experience all eight components in a meaningful way, the parish is effectively reaching the three goals as spelled out by the bishops.

Forming a
Good Strategy

Perhaps a golf analogy might help us begin. There are many different approaches to playing the game of golf, but the game itself is the same for everyone. Every approach is inadequate, since the only perfect way to play golf would be to shoot an eighteen (a hole in one on every hole). That will never happen, nor would anyone want that to happen (what makes golf enjoyable is the prospect of improving). So golfers must constantly search for different ways, different approaches to the same game. So it is with youth ministry. If *Renewing the Vision* spells out for us what it is, then we must find ways in which to do it in the least inadequate way. There is no perfect strategy, but there must be an approach that works with greater consistency than all other approaches.

I contend that the place to start is by taking a look at two distinct but not separate models of faith formation. When combined and applied to *Renewing the Vision*, they form one clear and effective strategy for Catholic youth ministry. The two models are: Rite of Christian Initiation of Adults (RCIA—also known as the catechumenate), and Family-Based Faith Formation. When these two models are combined under the scope of *Renewing the Vision*, they provide the foundation

for what this book is calling an *Initiation Model of Youth Ministry*.

THE CATECHUMENATE PROCESS (RCIA)

(The following section is a summation of *The Rites of the Catholic Church Volume 1*, Forward and #1-35 of "Christian Initiation of Adults")

Since the Second Vatican Council decreed the restoration, revision, and adaptation of the catechumenate, this ancient practice of the Church has become *the* process through which we welcome adult converts into the Church.

It begins with a period of inquiry in which those seeking a faith community are warmly welcomed by the parish and are invited to "Come and See" what our Christian faith and Roman Catholic religious tradition are all about. More specifically, they are invited to inquire about becoming fully initiated members of the Catholic Church. If these inquirers accept the invitation to continue, they immediately move into the next period of formal catechesis and become candidates (if they have already been validly baptized) or catechumens (if they are un-baptized). Note that there is no academic calendar determining when one begins formal catechesis. They begin when they come forward, no matter what time of year.

FORMAL CATECHESIS

The period of formal catechesis could take years (depending on the individual's readiness), but usually takes about one year. When the candidates and catechumens are ready, they move into the third period of purification and enlightenment during Lent. "Readiness" is ultimately at the discretion of the pastor, but it is the parish community itself who journeys with the candidates and catechumens and accepts them into the different periods that determines readiness. The parish community does not just support the candidates and catechumens, but is expected to engage themselves into the lives of those who are seeking membership. In other words, the parish community as a whole initiates.

At the Easter Vigil, the candidates celebrate confirmation and First Eucharist (however, accepting candidates for full communion at the Easter Vigil along with catechumens is being discouraged in many dioceses in order to help stress the vigil's emphasis on baptism). The catechumens celebrate all three sacraments of initiation (baptism, confirmation, and Eucharist in that order). Once all are fully initiated, the neophytes (Greek word meaning "newly planted") then immediately enter into the final period of mystagogy (another Greek word meaning "grasping the mystery of God"), which extends throughout the Easter season and into the rest of their lives (all the fully initiated are constantly grasping the mystery of God ever more deeply).

> (The preceding is a summary of *The Rites of the Catholic Church*, Vol. 1, Forward and #1–35 of "Christian Initiation of Adults.")

The whole process is intertwined with the public work of the parish (i.e. liturgies, feast days, communal events, prayer services, outreach, retreats, etc.). In other words, the RCIA process coincides with the total "life of the parish." As Andre Aubrey writes, "In effect, the catechumenate is not a school, but an *initiation*. The school has some students who learn a lesson, initiation has some disciples who discover a life" (Aubrey, p. 180).

BREAKING OPEN THE WORD

In a typical RCIA process, the candidates and catechumens together with their sponsors and an RCIA team (consisting of parishioners), attend Sunday parish Mass for the Liturgy of the Word and are dismissed before the Liturgy of the Eucharist (except for candidates because they have already been invited to the table through baptism, in which case special arrangements would be made for the candidates to join the group after Mass). They gather together to break open the Word of Scripture and draw out from it our Catholic doctrine and tradition (all Catholic tradition is rooted in Scripture). This is called lectionary-based catechesis. It is catechesis that draws from the lectionary readings as it unfolds the story of who we are.

Throughout the whole process, there are different rites that are celebrated at weekend liturgies in order to mark the different stages of catechesis and conversion and in order to allow the parish community to be witnesses to the faith. The final rites being, of course, the rites of initiation (baptism, confirmation, and Eucharist) are celebrated at the Easter Vigil.

FAMILY-BASED FAITH FORMATION

This is an intergenerational process that encourages partnership between parish and home. It is a by-product of a new (or renewed) "whole church" paradigm in faith formation that is gaining momentum in the United States and Canada. In *Handbook for Success in Whole Community Catechesis*, Bill Huebsch explains in a sample bulletin announcement that "...in whole community catechesis, parents play a vital role alongside all the other members of the community....Added to that, whole community catechesis places great emphasis on developing households of faith" (Huebsch, p. 128).

One strategy used in this paradigm is the creation of opportunities for parents to participate in catechetical gatherings with their children, thus empowering them as the primary catechists and allowing them to foster their own ongoing conversion. For example, as an option for families, a parish might offer a monthly family-based gathering on a Sunday morning after Mass for parents to attend with their children. At the large group gathering, parents and their children participate in activities revolving around a lesson plan on a certain topic that flows out of the day's liturgy. The gathering can be structured in many different ways, but the overall emphasis is on "families learning together."

GENERATIONS OF FAITH

The Center for Ministry Development has offered us their *Generations of Faith* model, which is a superb resource for whole church faith formation and a comprehensive workbook for a family-based model. In the introduction to *Generations of Faith*, John Roberto describes how such a process continues outside the formal gathering:

> The catechetical task is to provide individuals and families with the resources and tools they need to extend and expand their learning from a preparation program and the experience of the event to their lives and home. We create event-specific home materials that help families and individuals celebrate traditions and rituals, continue their learning, pray together, serve others and work for justice, and enrich their relationships and family life. Attention to home resources and tools is as important as the parish preparation program. (Roberto, Section I, Vision and Practice, p. 20)

Family-based faith formation is taking on many different forms in parishes throughout North America; however, what they all have in common is the belief that education is not just for children and that it takes a whole church to form faith. The classroom is only one area among many where people learn, and since the Church has always taught that parents are the primary faith givers family-based models are structured to empower parents and provide them with the tools they need to continue religious education in the home and in life.

Both the RCIA and family-based models of faith formation have proven over the years to be successful and life-giving; however, this success need not be limited to specific ministries. For example, lectionary-based catechesis is not limited to the RCIA process, but can be the norm for the faith formation of all ministerial processes. Family-based faith formation is proving to be more than just an option for young parents, but also a permanent expectation of all families.

In other words, these two models can and have been combined to form a new model, a new way if you will, of doing youth ministry, and it works! With *Renewing the Vision* as the framework, I believe that combining the RCIA (or catechumenate) and family-based strategies to adolescent faith formation is the most consistent (or if you prefer, least inadequate) means through which to reach the three goals of youth ministry in a post-modern Church. We are calling it an *Initiation Model of Youth Ministry.*

 # An Initiation Model

One way in which the Encarta dictionary (easily accessed by my computer) defines the word "initiation" is "a usually secret or mysterious ceremony by which somebody is admitted to a group, organization, or religion." I think that most Americans conjure this type of image when presented with the word "initiation."

Initiation theology within our Church, however, is something very different. It speaks of an agenda that is not secret but very public. It is mysterious only in the sense that it tries to tap into the mystery of God. It is ongoing, open to all, person-centered, process-oriented, and follows the sequence of the Church calendar.

Robert Duggan describes in an article in *New Theology Review* how his parish tries to implement initiation theology in all that it does:

> Preparation for the sacrament of baptism, confirmation, first Eucharist, first reconciliation, and marriage all follow a "catechumenal model" that is gradual, progressive, developmentally sensitive, and wherever possible family-centered and intergenerational. Commitment, conversion, intentional faith, and such

terms aptly describe the "hidden agenda" of all learning in these diverse contexts.... We strive to make it clear that learning about one's faith is a lifelong process that does not end with confirmation, that our Catholic faith involves moral imperatives, that participation in worship has pedagogical dimensions and ethical implications, and that a praxis of service both within and beyond the Christian community is the natural correlate of one's baptism into discipleship. (Duggan, "Parish as a Center...", p. 18)

What distinguishes this book from most youth ministry strategy books is that it does not rely on a classroom model as the basis for the structure or curriculum, even when youth ministry is called on to prepare young people for confirmation.

THE PARISH IS THE STRUCTURE

In an Initiation Model of Youth Ministry, the parish itself is the structure and the people are the witnessing faith-sharers. So technically, there is a curriculum or a "structure," but it is not expressed or taught in the "traditional" way. The "structure" is best described as "the life of the parish," or as Maria Harris puts it: "the entire course of the Church's life" (Harris, p. 63). This "life" is centered on Eucharist and committed to an ongoing and deepening relationship in the way of Christ.

This way to do youth ministry is really not new. In fact, the revised *General Directory for Catechesis* has already stated that the catechumenate "is the model of [the Church's] catechizing activity" (#90). What an Initiation Model essentially does then is take the catechumenate model, as is called for by the *General Directory* and make appropriate adaptations in order to be consistent with *Renewing the Vision* (which recognizes the primacy of family). Therefore, the catechumenate model is not only applied to the catechesis of adolescents, but is applied to their evangelization, community life, pastoral care, justice and service, prayer and worship, leadership development, and advocacy.

Furthermore, the premise for an Initiation Model is firmly rooted in the teachings, beliefs, and tradition of the Roman Catholic Church.

"The parish initiates the Christian people into the ordinary expression of the liturgical life."
Catechism of the Catholic Church, #2179

For young people to be initiated "into the ordinary expression of the liturgical life," the parish community must be a place and a people through which this happens. In a sense, everyone who shows up at Mass on Sunday is responsible for showing one another, especially our young people, how to liturgically express our faith and our gratitude in and toward our God. If everyone walked into the church building with this in mind, imagine what our liturgies would be like!

"Catechesis is an *education in the faith* of children, young people, and adults which includes especially the teaching of Christian doctrine imparted, generally speaking, in an organic and systematic way, with a view

to initiating the hearers into the fullness of Christian life."
Catechism of the Catholic Church, #5

Catechesis "in an organic and systematic way" implies that in order to initiate our young people "into the fullness of Christian life," we are to impart Christian doctrine in a way that relates to people's everyday lives and in a way that is an organized process designed to propel one forward. The liturgical cycle of our Church is both organic and systematic. It has a natural flow that is the ground for the life of the parish and is an organized process that takes us through the life, death, and resurrection of Jesus Christ. The parish community is the primary place and people through which the liturgical cycle is experienced and through which our young people are initiated into true discipleship.

"One of the highest responsibilities of the people of God is to prepare the baptized for confirmation."
Rite of Confirmation, Introduction #3

How do the people of God prepare young people for confirmation? Answer: Through witness. The people of God (young and old) are given the opportunity to pass on our faith through the structure and community of their parish. In other words, in order for a young person to be fully initiated into the Catholic Church, he or she must experience the witness of the whole parish community, not just catechists and youth ministers.

"The parish community has a special role in promoting participation in the life, mission, and work of the faith community."
Renewing the Vision, p. 13

Whether preparing to be initiated or already fully initiated, participation in the faith community is always the expectation. But this expectation is only communicated to our young people when the parish community at large is an active one.

Finally, as mentioned earlier, much has already been written on the broader topic of "whole church" faith formation by educators like Maria Harris, Bill Huebsch, and John Roberto. Even though these authors do not go so far as to formally declare their work as by-products of initiation theology, I and others in pastoral ministry, like Robert Duggan, Thomas Ivory, and Thomas Zanzig do suggest that this is precisely where "whole church" faith formation finds its roots.

> The initiatory strategy, which weds formal catechesis to ritual celebration, intensive interactions with an intergenerational faith community, opportunities of witness and service, and various other formative experiences, complements and integrates lectionary-based catechesis in a balanced and holistic manner. (Robert D. Duggan, "Lectionary-based Catechesis," p. 20)

> The period of the actual catechumenate can last for several years, and the New Rite of Christian Initiation envisions a multi-dimensional catechesis. This involves: 1) doctrinal formation accommodated to the liturgical year; 2) experience of Christian community, in which the catechumens are formed by living closely with others who are trying to live the Christian way of life; 3) participation in public worship, especially the Liturgy of the Word; and 4) apostolic involvement, working actively with others to spread the gospel and build up the Church by the testimony of their lives and the profession of their faith. Such catechesis obviously goes beyond the confines of a classroom or a discussion group and hold forth great possibilities for ministry by many members of the parish community. (Thomas P. Ivory, p. 228)

> The focus and concern in initiation is as much on the life of the entire community into which the candidate is being initiated as on the individual being initiated, if not more so....The heart of the initiation process is located not in a religious education classroom but in the life of the total faith community. (Thomas Zanzig, p. 28)

WHAT'S AT WORK

Many parishes have already put "whole church" theory into practice and have recognized that initiation theology is really what is at work. It is not only applied when preparing for and celebrating the three sacraments of initiation, but is applied as a model for parish life as a whole. This is because initiation theology goes right to the heart of what it means to be a parish. The initiation parish acknowledges that everyone is on a faith journey at all points in life and that it is the role of every member of Christ's Body (the Church) to help one another grow more deeply into the mystery of God. It is based on "relationship" that is grounded on the practice of "listening before responding."

CENTERED ON EUCHARIST

This kind of operative theology, however, needs to have a source (a place *from* which to flow) and a summit (a place *toward* which to grow); and therefore the initiation parish begins and ends with Eucharist. *Everything that the initiation parish does is focused on gathering at table to be sent outside in mission, which leads one right back to gathering at table.* It is much like a dance. The real presence of Jesus is celebrated at Mass so that all can *be* the real presence of Jesus out in the world, which quite naturally leads one right back to Mass to celebrate the real presence of Jesus within the community.

Hence, an Initiation Model of Youth Ministry is centered on Eucharist. Everything that youth ministry does within this model flows *from* Mass and *toward* mission, and *back* to Mass, constantly repeating those three steps over and over again in the never-ending dance.

It has the same goals as spelled out in *Renewing the Vision*, and it creates opportunities for young people and their families to experience all eight components of youth ministry. *However, what makes this model of youth ministry unique is that everything is structured as a direct response to what we do and experience at Mass.* "We eat the Body of Christ to become the Body of Christ" (St. Augustine).

There is not a catechetical gathering, a service opportunity, a leadership role, or a prayer service that is not in some way connected to the Sunday Eucharist. Any participation in youth ministry would be incomplete and out of context if one has not first fully, consciously, and actively celebrated Eucharist with the parish community.

STRUCTURED BACKWARDS

Most youth ministry models, I believe, are structured backwards. Programs are created within the eight components that try to encourage young people and their families to go to Mass. But this approach, as I see it, is not working in the long run. For instance, many young people show up for confirmation class on a Sunday night without having celebrated Eucharist earlier that day. The class becomes in their minds, "the Sunday obligation." Some parishes have tried to combat this problem by scheduling catechetical efforts directly after or before Mass. This is closer to being on the right track, but no matter what the parish does, taking a "Eucharist flowing from youth ministry" approach is a losing battle because the experience of worship on that day is disconnected from what is experienced at the gathering. Youth ministry, as all parish ministry, must flow from Eucharist, not vice versa.

For example, suppose St. Will's Parish has scheduled a ninth and tenth grade youth ministry gathering on the evening of the Epiphany of the Lord. Concerned about Mass attendance, the parish decides to end the gathering with a closing Sunday liturgy. The topic for the evening is "The Beatitudes." So as one can imagine, the gathering is full of reflections and discussions and presentations on the Sermon on the Mount. But when the closing liturgy begins, all hear about the Magi following the star and the infant Christ who has come to save all peoples. The Mass becomes a "sidebar" for the whole evening. It is billed as a closing celebration for a youth ministry event but has no real connection to that event. This is backward.

If St. Will's Parish wants to cover the topic of the beatitudes, it would be better suited if the topic flowed out of Eucharist. For example, the Fourth Sunday in Ordinary Time (Year A) and the Sixth Sunday in Ordinary Time (Year C) are both Sundays when the beatitudes are proclaimed. With this example, the people can now at least connect the message at Mass with something they have already discussed. All components of youth ministry are clearly connected to the experience at Mass and can now flow back into it.

BACK TO EUCHARIST

In an Initiation Model, the celebration of Eucharist encourages or sends forth young people and their families to participate in programs within youth ministry (mission), which directs them in turn to dance their way back into Eucharist. It looks to the ancient initiation processes and rituals of the Church as a guide toward authentic Christian conversion (conversion is not limited to the unbaptized, but is ongoing for all Christians, even the fully initiated ones). "The liturgy is the summit toward which the activity of the Church is directed; at the same time it is the fount from which all the Church's power flows. It is therefore the privileged place for catechizing the People of God" (*Catechism of the Catholic Church*, #1074).

The lectionary is the current on which all Catholics flow. The Jesus story is revealed to us through the three-year cycle, and so *our* story is revealed; therefore, an initiation model uses a lectionary-based approach to all eight components of youth ministry, especially catechesis. This approach allows adolescents and their families to travel with the rest of the parish through the liturgical seasons and connects them to the universal Church. They come to know Jesus as the story of revelation is unfolded for them and broken open with them week after week.

Like the RCIA process, this model of youth ministry includes the whole parish, calling all parishioners to initiate one another and engage themselves in the lives of the young people. It acknowledges that the three goals of youth ministry cannot be met by simply attending all of the required catechism classes or by attending a weekly youth group social. Conversion is the aim, and a single-faceted youth ministry will not cut it.

AN ONGOING PROCESS

There is no "one size fits all" in this model. Not everyone experiences Christian conversion at the same time or in the same way. Full participation in the life of the parish is the journey for all parishioners, young and old. Conversion is an ongoing process and is lifelong, thus too big for a "youth program" or a "confirmation program." Through intergenerational and age-appropriate opportunities within the eight components, young people may journey at their own pace within the natural flow of the Church calendar, moving cyclically with the invitation of growing deeper and deeper in the mystery of God. The parish community is entrusted, as it has been for centuries, to be the instrument through which this takes place. Whether senior high youth are preparing for confirmation or have already been confirmed, the conversion process will always be ongoing and different for all, and therefore requires a comprehensive youth ministry strategy that can adapt.

PRIMACY OF FAMILY

However, let us not forget that it is primarily the responsibility of parents within the parish community to foster conversion within the life of their children.

> The initiation of children into the sacramental life is ordinarily the responsibility and concern of Christian

parents. They are to form and gradually increase a spirit of faith in the children and, at times with the help of catechism classes, prepare them for the fruitful reception of the sacraments of confirmation and Eucharist. The role of the parents is also expressed by their active participation in the celebration of the sacraments. (*The Rite of Confirmation*, Introduction #3)

The home is the domestic church, the "first and vital cell of society," the primary educator of faith and virtues. Since the family is the first place where ministry to adolescents usually occurs, the Church is at the service of parents to help them enliven within their children a knowledge and love for the Catholic faith. (*Renewing the Vision*, p. 21)

PRACTICE CHANGES

There was a time when I was perplexed by how the religious practice of most young people changes dramatically when they enter college or young adulthood. Take Laura as an example. She had a profound conversion during her sophomore year of high school when she participated in the Antioch Retreat. Suffice it to say that the retreat accomplished for her what it was structured to do: make disciples. Ever since that retreat, Laura involved herself in youth ministry as much as possible. She came to Mass every week (even though her parents did not). She even became one of youth ministry's strongest peer leaders as a junior and senior. On the surface, it seemed that the three goals of youth ministry were definitely being met, at least in Laura's case. But when she went away to college, she, like most people her age, took a vacation from her religion. Four years of college went by and then four more years of post-college went by, and Laura did not set foot in church. She still had faith in God and always looked back on her time in youth ministry with much fondness, but she had no desire to express her faith through

MANY LIKE THIS.

the Roman Catholic tradition anymore. What happened?

Answer: As an adolescent, Laura had a connection with her religious tradition, but it was not nourished by those in her family. Her primary faith-givers never experienced for themselves a lasting connection to their religious tradition and, perhaps for many reasons, did not involve themselves in their parish, even when Laura did. The youth ministry that Laura experienced was excellent except for one thing: it never invited parents to do anything more than drop their teens off and pick them up. Eventually I came to realize that even the best youth ministry in the world couldn't keep Laura connected in the long run because her parents were connected to the parish in name only.

A DOOMED PROCESS

Any parish model that is structured without giving parents the opportunity to live out their role as the primary faith-givers is doomed to create teens who only temporarily involve themselves in the life of the Church. Of course, there are always those who somehow make it and become active members of the Church even without parent witness, but we all know that those are the exceptions.

The National Study of Youth and Religion recently published *Soul Searching: The Religious and Spiritual Lives of American Teenagers* by Christian Smith with Melinda Lundquist Denton. In the survey, the authors confirm what many of us already know: the immediate and long-term religious beliefs and practices of teenagers are heavily influenced by their parents. The religious practice (or lack thereof) of their parents will more times than not become their own religious practice during and after adolescence.

SUPPORTING PARENTS

An Initiation Model recognizes that "faith is caught, not taught." Parents are and will always be on the front lines of passing on our tradition.

They are the primary "catchers of faith," but too often in youth ministry, parents are not given the tools or the opportunities to share their faith with their teens. Sometimes we in church leadership even take the attitude that we are not responsible for creating opportunities for parents to share their faith with their children because we falsely believe that they should figure that out on their own.

Often it seems that a parish youth ministry is structured in a way that is almost reluctant to include parents in the process. Most of the time, this reluctance is out of fear of adult relationships or that young people will not be responsive if their parents are present and vice versa.

This model transcends those fears and supports parents as they live out the promises they made at their child's baptism. It provides parents with a venue and the tools to share their faith with their teens in a meaningful way.

Overall, we will do well in youth ministry if we immerse ourselves in initiation theology and look to family-based models and to the early Church as an example of what "whole church" faith formation is all about.

> We can clearly see what great emphasis there was on the community aspect of initiation. The community sponsored the candidates, instructed them, prayed for them, and assembled to greet them and welcome them after baptism. The community, in a word, was quite active. It was reaching out and giving the first centuries' equivalent of "welcome," and it was not only a welcome in the sense that one is now a part of the community, but welcome also in the sense that the community would be there in the ongoing process of becoming a Christian. Baptism was only the beginning. (William J. Bausch, *A New Look at the Sacraments*, p. 61)

Thomas Zanzig's *Confirmed in a Faithful Community* is a good seminal work on applying initiation theology to senior high youth ministry. Later in this book, we will use and build upon some of the structure and terminology that Zanzig suggests. Although Zanzig cautions that "we must accept the fact that our task is to gently and patiently lead our parishes step-by-step toward a deeper understanding and actual practice of this vision of initiation" (Zanzig, p. 29), we will not be so cautious in this book. The time has come for an Initiation Model to be foundational to all areas of parish life, including youth ministry. As a result, we, the Church, will be able to foster environments where family experience and parish experience only strengthen the connection to our religious tradition. The early Christians knew this and practiced this. So shall we.

SECTION TWO

HOW TO STRUCTURE A PARISH-BASED YOUTH MINISTRY THAT WORKS

 # Lessons Learned

F ourteen years ago, with the emergence of a new youth minister (me), my home parish decided to make a major paradigm shift in its approach to the sacrament of confirmation. (In our diocese, confirmation is celebrated in the sophomore or junior year of high school.) This shift was primarily a shift from a textbook-based catechesis to a lectionary-based catechesis. We tried to introduce the youth and their families to a structure based on the RCIA model. We envisioned a ministry that did not resemble school, but "emphasized (trans)formation in addition to religious literacy" (Duggan, "Parish as a Center...", p. 14). That same year, the U.S. bishops published *Renewing the Vision*, and we embraced that vision. We viewed the adaptation of the RCIA model and the family-based model as the best and most effective means through which we could accomplish the goals set forth by that document. So I began my ministry within this new model that was more consistent with the vision of the U.S. bishops.

It was a major struggle at first. I was trying to learn a great deal in a short period of time. Of course, I had a great personality (at least my mom thinks so!), the teens liked me for the most part, and ministry came naturally to me, but truthfully,

I didn't know the first thing about RCIA and how to adapt it to youth ministry. As a result, the new model of youth ministry was having a hard time distinguishing itself from any classroom-based model. Although we were using phrases like, "it's a process, not a program," and "confirmation is a beginning, not an ending," and we were using a lectionary-based approach, our new model still had many elements of the old model: required attendance at confirmation class; required to come to a make-up class if you missed; youth-only Masses that separated the youth from the rest of the parish; parents signing a contract that stated that anyone missing more than two sessions would be forced to postpone the sacrament for a year; making youth prove that they did the required amount of service, etc. We were using initiation words, but we still were not initiating.

A DECISION MADE

After five years of trial and error, at long last we decided to go all the way with the initiation approach. Realizing that experience leads to understanding, we did away with the "one size fits all" confirmation classes. We put the emphasis on four years of youth ministry, rather than two years of confirmation preparation. We concentrated on improving our retreat processes, stressing ongoing, lectionary-based, weekly follow-up gatherings (a weekly gathering or reunion of candidates and team who participated in a retreat together). We improved and emphasized our outreach, providing an abundance of service opportunities. We finally began to live up to the realization that strong ritual, carefully prepared and celebrated well, remains the primary "school of faith" for most Catholics including our youth (Duggan, "Parish as a Center…", p. 14), and consequently more youth began to celebrate Eucharist more frequently. We improved and emphasized liturgical rites that marked the different stages of faith formation and included the whole parish. We took a more family-based approach to catechesis, especially in the preparation for the different rites. The role of the parents was supported as they accepted the challenge of ownership and responsibility for it. The "Youth Mass" went by the wayside, and the regular 12:00 parish Mass was given a youthful feel. Overall, we created a youth ministry through which our young people and their families could experience all eight components as spelled out by our bishops.

These steps were taken because our vision of initiation youth ministry suddenly came into focus. We knew that everything we did had to be consistent with everything we believed parish youth ministry to be. So what did we believe? What does initiation theology have to say about youth ministry?

 # Fundamental Beliefs

1. Youth ministry is not a program. It just is! It is a lived experience of the parish: a lived experience of the gospel and the Catholic tradition. Programs have beginnings and endings. Youth ministry has no beginning and no end. (Yes, I know, we all have calendars and must start somewhere, but keep reading!) Youth ministry, for all intents and purposes, *is ongoing faith formation through which youth and their families live out their baptismal call within the life of the parish.* Every retreat, every service opportunity, every prayer experience, every catechetical experience, every worship experience is part of total youth ministry. When youth ministry is seen as a "program," it can very easily separate itself from the rest of the parish. It becomes a separate entity that often does not share the same vision as the parish at large. Programs tend to stop and then start up again. Youth ministry should never stop. Furthermore, it is not seen as a separate group in the parish. It is just one ministry within a parish structure that is primarily designed for youth and their families; however, all parishioners are touched by youth ministry in some way.

Example: The second parish that employed me as their director had no real youth ministry in place when I arrived. What they did have was a few different programs that included youth, such as a confirmation class program, a homeless outreach program, and an Appalachia summer outreach program. These were all separate, each with its own coordinator and regular volunteers.

Consequently, the young people and their parents never really viewed participation in a program as only one aspect of a greater vision. If one wanted to prepare for confirmation, one would be in the confirmation program. If one wanted to help others, one would join an outreach effort. When the program was over, that was it: wait until next year for the program to start up again.

One of my first jobs was to restructure all of these realities so that it was clear to everyone, especially the coordinators and regular volunteers, that any participation in any of these areas of parish life was in fact a response to Eucharist and therefore participation in parish youth ministry. When a new youth ministry sponsored event or program was later added on, it was always made clear that it was a part of a greater youth ministry effort. Making the paradigm shift from program to lived experience is still something that many young people and parents are struggling with in that particular parish. It does not happen overnight, especially in a culture that is entrenched in a program mentality. But strides have been and are continuing to be made.

2. Confirmation preparation (if celebrated during the high school years) is not separate from youth ministry but is a part of senior high youth ministry, which is part of the entire parish. The parish is responsible for creating a youth ministry through which every adolescent can experience age-appropriate faith formation no matter when confirmation is celebrated. In other words, it is like a formational "chicken and the egg." When confirmation is celebrated at a high-school level, the preparation *is* participation in youth ministry, and participation in youth ministry *is* confirmation preparation. Likewise, post-confirmation mystagogy *is* participation in youth ministry and vice versa. Of course, for those preparing for confirmation, there are additional "confirmation specific" events, such as rites of passage and sacramental catechesis, but the parish's senior high youth ministry would generally look the same whether confirmation is celebrated at a high school level or not.

Example: When we first decided to go all the way with the Initiation approach, we discontinued our monthly confirmation sessions for numerous reasons. One of the major reasons was that the monthly sessions on the calendar communicated that confirmation preparation is something other than youth ministry. In the minds of most families, there was confirmation class (that lasted two years), and there was youth ministry. Both were separate things. So we simply stopped having confirmation sessions. We no longer had a confirmation registration form, but a youth ministry registration form. There was no longer a fee for the program, but a requested donation to the ministry. We said to the youth and their parents that we simply have a comprehensive youth ministry that provides opportunities for them to experience all eight components within the parish and that most of those opportunities were age appropriate and intergenerational.

We further communicated that the opportunities that we provided were designed for freshmen through seniors and that youth ministry does not end with confirmation. We trusted that parents would take it upon themselves to monitor their own teen's involvement and make sure that it was well balanced and sufficient. Some of my colleagues in nearby parishes thought that we were being very brave and were skeptical about how it would play out. There were questions about how we would know if someone had enough catechesis. How would we be sure that we would have enough income? What if someone came forward for confirmation without having been sufficiently prepared? What if they didn't go on a retreat or do any service? There was nothing quantifiable, and that notion scared the heck out of some.

MORE FAMILIES REGISTERED

Here is the truth about what happened: Each year after the change, more and more families with confirmed juniors and seniors registered for youth ministry even though there was no perceived obligation to do so. The parish actually took in more income with a general request for a donation than with a fixed registration fee. Some young people who would have done the minimum requirements under the old model in order to be confirmed, wound up not being confirmed because both they and their parents knew for themselves that they did not take enough ownership. In other words, no one came forward for confirmation unless they knew in their hearts that they were sufficiently prepared for it. There wasn't one aspect of youth ministry that was considered to be "painful" by either the adults involved or the young people, because whatever the event, people for the most part wanted to be there (the old confirmation sessions were indeed painful, and making the young people sit through them was borderline child abuse!).

The number of young people interested in liturgical ministry and peer leadership increased dramatically. The summer outreach program became so popular that we had to schedule three different trips. Mass attendance among young people and their families was becoming noticeably more frequent. Finally, by the end of the fifth year of working from this model, eighty percent of confirmed juniors and seniors were still active in youth ministry. Was it perfect? Not by any stretch of the imagination. We definitely lost some families who would have jumped through the confirmation requirement hoops, but it was a necessary loss. Sometimes, like Jesus, we in church leadership are going to encounter people who cannot bring themselves to a point of intentional and committed discipleship. Although it is sad to let them walk away, it is better than confirming people whose faith is not intentional.

3. Membership in parish is defined by participation.

We are all called to serve our brothers and sisters. As baptized Christians and as Catholics, we believe that our membership in the Body of Christ is defined by how we treat each other. "Amen, I say to you, whatever you did for one of these least brothers and sisters of mine, you did for me" (Matthew 25:40). Whether one is preparing for confirmation or is already confirmed, all baptized parishioners are invited into active participation in the life of the parish. One role of parish leadership is to empower every parishioner (including youth) to be active in some way. This suggests that attendance at Mass is simply not enough.

Celebrating Eucharist is only one part of Eucharist. "Going in peace to love and serve the Lord" is the other major part that may often be overlooked by many Catholics. Stewardship (time, talent, and treasure) applies just as much to young people as it does to adult parishioners. If a family registers for youth ministry, the expectation is that they will take advantage of the myriad of opportunities to live out Christianity through the

Roman Catholic Tradition that the parish provides. The goals of youth ministry cannot even begin to be met until young people freely share the gift of themselves within the parish community, not because of requirement, obligation, or cultural pressure, but because of a clear understanding of Christian mission.

Example: For the past twenty summers, my home parish has sent youth and adult parishioners to a section of West Virginia to spend a week renovating dilapidated homes owned by our brothers and sisters who are dealing with the unfortunate situation of rural poverty. This effort is a partnership between our parish and the Catholic parish that is responsible for ministering to that particular county in West Virginia. The night of our arrival, there is a traditional orientation meeting run by the leaders of the West Virginia parish. Part of the orientation is asking for a volunteer who has participated in this trip before to stand up and share why he or she has returned.

Most people share that they like helping others, that they learned a lot from previous experiences, and that they believe that it is good for them to see poverty firsthand (which is a reason that drives me nuts, but that's another story). Then one year, one of the young adult volunteers who had been coming every year since she was in high school stood up and shared with us what I believe sums up what Christian mission is all about. She said that she returns year after year because she has to, but not out of guilt or pity. She is obligated to return and serve her brothers and sisters because she feels incomplete if she does not. "I have to serve others in order to be whole," she said. She went on to say that she feels like she is most a part of her parish when she is serving on that trip.

That young woman knew that participating in that outreach effort year after year wasn't just a good thing to do, but made her a complete Christian. She views her membership in the parish and consequently the Church as defined by what she does. The young people who heard that witness still talk about it.

4. Experience leads to learning. As Michael Himes writes:

> One does not know and then do. After all, if you had to understand the doctrine and mystery of the Eucharist correctly before you celebrated and participated in it, which one of us would have ever received our first communions? (*Doing the Truth in Love*, p. 20)

The experience of being a Catholic Christian always comes before learning the doctrines of our faith. Young people are always more open to learning our faith when they first have a faith experience. It's makes little sense to me to try to teach Church doctrine to people who have not yet had a profound faith experience. When such an attempt is made, it usually ends up with the teacher and student both having huge headaches. The student doesn't want to hear it because his/her life experience has yet to provide a context for the teaching. The teacher dreads it because it is like trying to feed a horse who isn't hungry. Only after one is aware that he/she has encountered Jesus, will one ever decide to actively learn about the teachings of Jesus. When one has the opportunity to hear and experience the faith stories of the *whole parish community*, one is then ready to get knee deep into understanding the doctrines of our Faith. Experience leads to learning.

Example: Almost all catechists would agree that young people respond much better to catechetical efforts after a good retreat experience than before the retreat. On a good retreat, they hear and experience the faith stories of their peers (and hopefully some adults as well). The sharing that takes place on a retreat is not unlike the sharing that takes place at the Eucharistic table, but this connection between life and ritual could never be understood and made real unless one is first awakened to the presence of God within life experience. Only after experiencing the sharing that occurs on a retreat or something similar does the young person even have a chance of making the connection between liturgical ritual and the way we live our lives. Most retreat models refer to this as the "Jesus Encounter." Participants experience Jesus in the midst of the people on the retreat and therefore have some kind of conversion. Through experience they have discovered what life as a Christian is all about.

5. Quality is much more important than quantity. "How many kids do you have in your youth group?" I get this question all of the time. In our culture, we tend to see greater numbers as synonymous with success: the bigger the youth group, the stronger the youth ministry. This could not be farther from the truth. Technically, there should not be one "youth group." There is simply a youth ministry that is designed to provide opportunities for the young people of the parish and their families to live out their baptismal call. These opportunities are planned and scheduled with a deliberate process in mind and with great attention to detail. Nothing is done to fill a quota or to simply just say that we did it. Do everything well, and the numbers will take care of themselves.

Example: It was the first year in which youth ministry attempted to lead the parish in a Living Stations of the Cross on the evening of Good Friday. It had never been attempted before, so there was concern if we would get enough actors, and if we did, if anyone would show up. Nonetheless, we gave it a shot. It was Year B in the Church calendar so the main resource that we used was Fr. Eugene LaVerdiere's *Way of the Cross according to Mark* from Emmanuel Publishing (which, by the way, I highly recommend as well as his other versions according to Matthew, Luke, John, and Paul). We were only able to get six young people and one adult to commit to it; however, those seven people understood that if they were going to do it, they were going to do it to the best of their ability.

LEARNING TOOK PLACE

We practiced for an hour and a half every Thursday night for eight weeks. In the process, the seven learned a great deal about this ancient prayer tradition. We decided to enhance the prayer experience with music, incense, costumes, slides, a spotlight, and even a light show. When Good Friday arrived, those seven committed people led what turned out to be an extremely moving and powerful prayer experience. Unfortunately, only about forty people showed up (most of whom were family). Was it all worth it? Absolutely! Forty-seven people were touched by that experience. Even if no one showed up on Good Friday, it would have been worth it because of the quality of the experience. Besides, word about the quality of the prayer spread quickly, and by the third year, we had more volunteers than parts and a full church showing up on Good Friday.

6. There is a clear distinction between faith and religion. Faith is one's belief in God, and religion is the way in which one expresses his/her faith. This distinction is important because faith is more the focus than religion during junior high and the first two years of senior high youth ministry. Specifically, during freshman and sophomore year of high school, the focus is more on Christianity and what it means to be a Christian than on Catholicism and what it means to be a Catholic. *This does not mean that our Roman Catholic religious tradition is ignored!* Certainly, all of youth ministry in the parish is done through the Roman Catholic tradition. This simply means that forming disciples through experiencing the Roman Catholic tradition is the focus rather than teaching Church doctrine as a means to deposit faith upon individuals. One must be able to accept and embrace the Christian faith before one can accept and embrace the Catholic religion. *One must become a disciple before one becomes a theologian.* We who coordinate youth ministry in parishes must understand that the majority of thirteen- to fifteen-year-olds are developmentally unable to

fully embrace a religious tradition. For most people of this age, *fully* embracing a religious tradition, any religion, is unrealistic.

CAN'T DESCRIBE FAITH

We know through James Fowler's work that young people of this age have a "Synthetic Conventional Faith." They know what faith is but cannot describe it. To a freshman or sophomore, God is interpersonal. Any sense of interpersonal betrayal can have him/her doubting his/her belief in God. At this stage of faith, God can become a compensatory being. In other words, freshmen and sophomores will typically believe that they can flee to God, but God is not present to them every day. Furthermore, due to their stage of development, freshmen and sophomores have an extremely fettered image of God. They are unable to image the true living God because there are too many distractions from the superego. John J. Shea describes this in his article "The Superego God."

> In fettered imaging, *it is not that reality is not grasped at all*; it is simply that *reality is imaged in a fettered way.* It is as if there were a veil or a grid on reality, providing still-forming and immature images of the real. It is not, therefore, that adolescing selves (teenagers) have no religious experience; often they have religious experiences in the early years which are profound and lasting. It is, rather, that their continuous imaging of God is going to be influenced to some extent by the workings of the superego. (Shea, p. 339)

It is completely natural for underclassers to have a fettered image of God; however, if they are unable to unfetter their image of God as they move toward adulthood, their faith development will come to a standstill, and they will be unable to image the true living God. They will continue to image a superego God; that is, a supreme being God with all power, a God of law who commands what must and must not be done, a God of belief who gives propositions about what must and must not be accepted as true, a God of dependency and control who holds us back from self-actualization, and a God of the group who would have us conform and who would directly appoint certain individuals from the group to have authority (Shea, *Finding Faith Again*, pp. 23-31).

FAITH BEFORE RELIGION

This is why faith must always come before religion, especially at this crucial developmental stage. Our Church must be consistent with the developmental reality that teenagers in our culture are not ready to *reflectively* look at life's truths through symbolism and metaphor until approximately the age of 16-17 (Erikson). Freshmen and sophomores may grasp certain elements of our symbols, but they are still very much objective in their thinking. Because our religion is filled with the richness of symbols, "Catholicism" as a part of an educational curriculum or catechesis, is not stressed until the junior and senior years of high school which usually correspond with post-confirmation.

Example: When another youth minister colleague and I got together to discuss implementing a retreat process for juniors and seniors, we took a long look at what was out there. Both of our parishes already held homegrown freshmen retreat processes and the Antioch retreat process for sophomores. What was needed was a process that moved beyond the "Jesus Encounter" and delved more deeply into Sacred Tradition.

The problem we faced was that every retreat manual that we found dealt more with Christianity than it did with Catholicism. So, as often was the case in those years, we found ourselves creating a new retreat process from scratch. It did not take us long to realize that if Sacred Tradition and Church doctrine were to be the focus, we should go right to the source: the *Catechism of the Catholic Church*. We found that the four pillars of our tradition (the profession of faith, the celebration of the Christian mystery, life in Christ, and Christian prayer) actually provided a great structure and flow for the experience. Team leaders prepared witness talks on mystery, the Creed, the Lord's Prayer, the Liturgy of the Word, the Liturgy of the Eucharist, virtue-based morality, the communion of saints, and other topics that are a part of our tradition. Catechisms were given to candidates on the retreat, and through a question and answer activity, they learned how to use them.

AN IMMENSE DIFFERENCE

Essentially, what was discussed on the retreat and at the follow-up gatherings were all the things that we used to believe freshmen and sophomores had to know through confirmation class. The difference was immense. The confirmed juniors and seniors really wanted to know why "we the Church" believe what we do. They engaged themselves in conversation, asked good and interested questions (especially concerning why we believe what we believe), and reveled in the chance to theologize. The freshmen and sophomores, on the other hand, found it all rather boring and irrelevant to their lives and very seldom asked why we believe what we believe (out of indifference in my opinion).

Even though studies in faith development all suggested that freshmen and sophomores in high school are for the most part developmentally unable to see and understand truth in a subjective manner, we still tried to force feed them for years. Thank God we finally wised up when someone asked the question: "Why don't we focus on providing our freshmen and sophomores with faith experiences that will show them what it means to be Christian and wait until their junior and senior years to ask them to try to understand our Roman Catholic religious tradition?" It makes a lot of sense, but takes an enormous amount of courage for a parish to switch its focus from a religious education or confirmation preparation program to a four year senior high youth ministry process.

HOW TO STRUCTURE

So this then begs the question: "How do we structure parish youth ministry in such a way that it supports these beliefs?"

- First, we must define the different periods of the faith journey typical to the faith development of senior high adolescents.

- Second, we must provide age-appropriate and intergenerational experiences centered on Eucharist, designed around the eight components of youth ministry, and through which young people and their families can come to know Jesus the Risen Lord in the midst of the parish community.

- Third, we must bring to ritual the significant milestones of the journey through liturgical rites or ritual blessings (depending on whether or not confirmation preparation is a part of senior high youth ministry).

Completing these three steps with careful attention to detail and constant focus on Eucharist will indeed provide a youth ministry "wineskin" or structure that will be able to hold the "new wine" of initiation theology.

THE JOURNEY
OF FAITH

Every once in awhile, it is good to ask ourselves why we do what we do in order to avoid mindless routine. So here it goes: Why is it important to define different stages of the adolescent faith journey?

Answer: Because of the Bueller theory. Of course, I'm speaking about Ferris Bueller, the young "philosopher" from the movie *Ferris Bueller's Day Off* (played by Matthew Broderick) who rightfully states: "Life moves pretty fast. If you don't stop and look around once in a while, you could miss it."

It's hard to know where we're going in our faith journey if we don't pay attention to where we've been and where we are. Whether a parish celebrates the sacrament of confirmation at a senior high level or earlier, it is important to recognize, acknowledge, and celebrate these different stages as one moves toward an owned faith and beyond. By doing this, it makes the faith journey real for the young person and helps him/her have an awareness of how the Spirit is active in his/her life.

Moreover, youth ministry planners must understand adolescent faith development in order to provide age appropriate programming (remember that youth ministry as a whole is not a program, but programming exists within a youth ministry). By defining the different stages of the adolescent faith journey in an age-appropriate way, a parish can create programs under the umbrella of total Youth Ministry that best meet the needs of young people and best make *Renewing the Vision* a reality.

This notion, however, does pose some problems in respect to the centuries-old debate surrounding the three sacraments of initiation, in particular, the separation of baptism, confirmation, and Eucharist (theologically and chronologically).

A UNIFIED WHOLE

As the documents of Vatican II clearly remind us, the sacraments of initiation were always seen as a unified whole in the eyes of the early Church, celebrated together in one ritual by communities that prepared adult catechumens (the practice of infant baptisms did not become frequent until approximately the fifth century, and "age-of-reason" First Eucharist much later than that). At the Easter Vigil, these catechumens ritually committed to the faith with the Christian community as witness. The documents further declare that this unification and practice of adult initiation is indeed *normative* for the Church *today*, but as we know in the Western Church, the separation of the three sacraments is practiced far more frequently and is usually completed no later than junior year of high school.

Because of this split in the Western Church, the sacrament of confirmation in particular has become labeled by many theologians as "the sacrament in search of a theology." It receives this dubious title because in baptism one commits to the faith and is anointed and becomes a new creation and has received all that is necessary for salvation, leaving confirmation with very little to distinguish itself as a separate source of grace.

It is not easy to distinguish between baptism and confirmation. Baptism is not merely a sacrament for the forgiveness of sins and for the acceptance of the individual into the church. It is also the sacrament of rebirth, of the grace-filled inner justification of man, the sacrament of the communication of the Spirit, without which the forgiveness of guilt, rebirth, and sanctification cannot even be received. And even if one stresses that in confirmation the Spirit is communicated to the recipient for particular tasks and special challenges, for a spiritual strengthening of the person to help him confess his faith before the world, it must be admitted that the Spirit received in baptism also confers on the individual the disposition and strength for undertaking special tasks. (Karl Rahner, *Confirmation Today*, p. 10)

If the society in which we now live is inimical to the growth of infant faith, we must surely question the expediency of infant baptism rather than try to twist the sacrament of confirmation into a second sacrament of commitment. (Austin P. Milner, *The Theology of Confirmation*, p. 105)

This poses the first problem for a youth ministry structure that seeks to define the different stages of the faith journey. If in baptism one has already theologically committed to the faith, how do we reconcile that with psychology, which suggests that one is developmentally unable to commit to a faith until late adolescence? If the sacrament of confirmation is celebrated during late adolescence, why not make it a declaration of an owned faith? But if we do, does that devalue and de-emphasize baptism?

My personal experience and education in confirmation has led me to side with those who believe that the best way to end the debate is to restore the unity of the initiation rite. As Bausch puts it:

> Either celebrate the entire baptism-confirmation-eucharist complex at infancy or enroll all infants in a catechumenate (remember, this is not a shameful downgrading: the catechumenate is a genuine, valid position in the church's tradition) and celebrate the rite later on in adolescence or adulthood. But keep the rite intact. (Bausch, p. 121)

If the latter is chosen, any dealings we have with confirmation will not "steal theology" from baptism, but will share it, as was originally the intention.

LESS THAN IDEAL

The Church's current position on confirmation, however, would suggest that no such measures will be taken anytime soon, so we are left with a less than ideal situation and are still presented with the first dilemma. Therefore, it

seems reasonable and helpful to me that if our Church insists on separating the sacraments of initiation—when that confirmation is administered during late adolescence—it certainly can't hurt to connect the choice to celebrate the sacrament with an awareness of an owned faith, as long as we are clear to catechize that the Spirit is received at baptism and has always been present and is now being confirmed. Said another way, it's not that the Holy Spirit was never there; rather, it's that one now recognizes that Spirit and chooses to acknowledge and celebrate the Spirit's presence in one's life through committing to an intentional faith. It is a re-commitment of the baptism that their parents chose for them. This obviously cannot be done by an infant or even a seventh grader. With this approach, we do not ignore or downplay baptism, rather, we constantly remind candidates about baptism and how it is calling them to own their faith. Confirmation then becomes (in one sense) a confirming of a faith that existed since baptism, but is now owned through full awareness.

A SECOND PROBLEM

We then have to deal with a second problem, particularly here in the United States, because although adolescent faith development is the same no matter where one lives, the sacrament of confirmation is not. For those parishes who celebrate confirmation within senior high adolescence, the opportunity is there to celebrate the sacrament (in one sense) as a confirmation of an owned faith. Those parishes who celebrate the sacrament before the high school years can't say this as readily, because as we have seen, such a declaration is simply not developmentally possible until later adolescence. Therefore, parishes that confirm during the high school years tend to define the faith journey differently from parishes whose senior high parishioners are already confirmed.

But let's go back to the original premise: teenagers are teenagers! Their faith development will be the same (for the most part) whether they are confirmed or not. Because an Initiation Model of Youth Ministry meets young people where they are, I propose that in both cases, we should define the journey of faith typical for senior high adolescents, stopping along the way to look around, while acknowledging where we are going. In this model, *the youth ministry process is the same for the confirmed youth and the "preparing to be confirmed" youth.* The only difference will be in sacramental theology. In a senior high youth ministry that celebrates confirmation, it is important to be consistent with catechumenate terminology (i.e. periods, rites, mystagogy, etc.) and to continuously highlight the anticipation of the sacrament that is alive in the individual; whereas with a senior high youth ministry that consists of confirmed youth, it is important to acknowledge that the grace of the sacrament has already been poured out and is alive within the young person, but at the same time, it is important to invite them to personally and publicly journey toward an owned faith.

So in both cases, the senior high faith journey can and should be defined, and most of the terminology will be the same.

VALID STAGES

Taking a cue from the RCIA model, an initiation model of senior high youth ministry defines seven stages of the adolescent faith journey that are valid and accurately describe the journeys for both confirmed and "preparing to be confirmed" senior high young people. For those preparing to be confirmed, we have placed these seven stages within five periods (in order to be more consistent with catechumenate terminology). Although certain personal situations may require a "tweaking" of the length of time in which one moves through each stage (i.e., a seventeen-year-old who decides to begin youth ministry during her junior year of high school), we are generally assuming here that the stages begin in ninth grade or fourteen years old and move through twelfth grade or eighteen years old:

Four Years of Senior High Youth Ministry with Confirmation

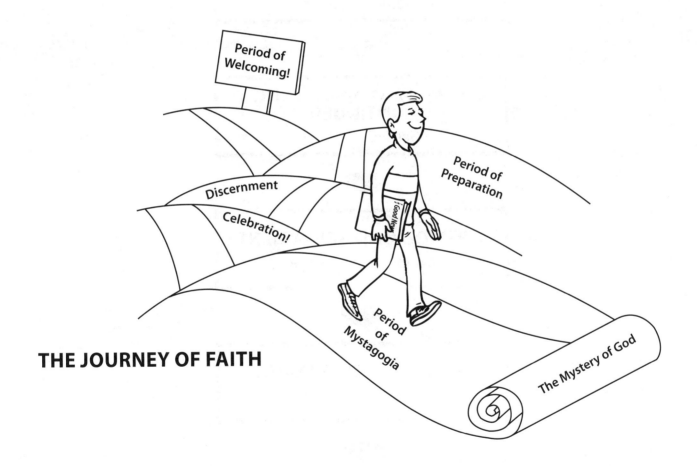

THE JOURNEY OF FAITH

1. PERIOD OF WELCOMING
Come and See Stage

2. PERIOD OF PREPARATION
Give It a Try Stage

3. PERIOD OF PREPARATION CONTINUED
Keep Going Stage

4. PERIOD OF PREPARATION CONTINUED
Get Serious Stage

5. PERIOD OF DISCERNMENT
Do You Believe? Stage

6. PERIOD OF CELEBRATION
I Believe Stage

7. PERIOD OF MYSTAGOGIA
Time and Talent Stage

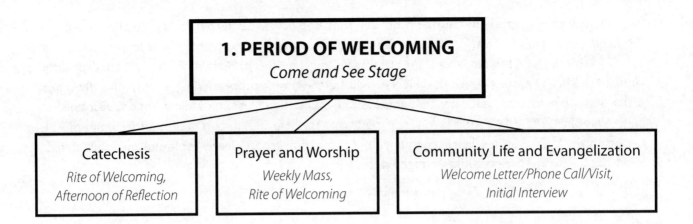

1. PERIOD OF WELCOMING
Come and See Stage

Catechesis
*Rite of Welcoming,
Afternoon of Reflection*

Prayer and Worship
*Weekly Mass,
Rite of Welcoming*

Community Life and Evangelization
*Welcome Letter/Phone Call/Visit,
Initial Interview*

During this period, young people are welcomed and invited to begin participation in senior high youth ministry. This period officially begins with the Rite of Welcoming celebrated within one or more of the parish's Sunday liturgies. After Mass, the young people and their parents are invited to spend a couple of hours at the church to learn about youth ministry and to build community. The gathering also serves as a chance for catechists to schedule initial interviews with the potential confirmation candidates. (Interviews can and should be scheduled with small groups of friends in order to avoid intimidation and on church property or in a public place so as to comply with "safe environment" guidelines.) This is preceded by a welcome letter and/or phone call and/or personal visit to both the parents and the potential candidates by the youth minister or whoever is responsible for coordinating the ministry. (See Appendices A, B, and C for examples of welcome letters and the initial interview.)

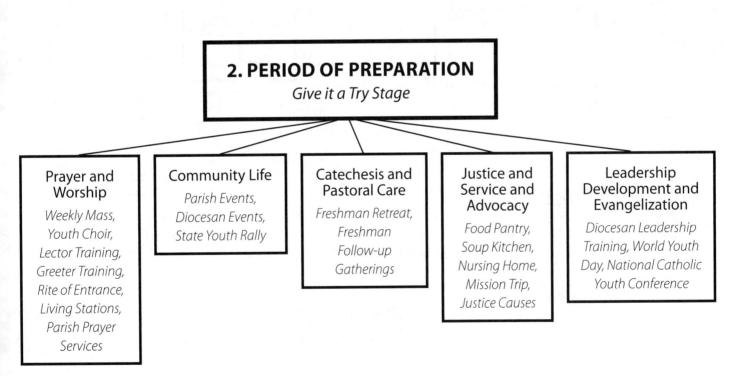

2. PERIOD OF PREPARATION
Give it a Try Stage

Prayer and Worship
*Weekly Mass,
Youth Choir,
Lector Training,
Greeter Training,
Rite of Entrance,
Living Stations,
Parish Prayer
Services*

Community Life
*Parish Events,
Diocesan Events,
State Youth Rally*

Catechesis and Pastoral Care
*Freshman Retreat,
Freshman
Follow-up
Gatherings*

Justice and Service and Advocacy
*Food Pantry,
Soup Kitchen,
Nursing Home,
Mission Trip,
Justice Causes*

Leadership Development and Evangelization
Diocesan Leadership Training, World Youth Day, National Catholic Youth Conference

Preparation officially begins for the individual when he or she participates in any aspect of parish youth ministry (outside of regular Sunday Mass). It can be different for each person (such as a parish trip to a soup kitchen, a parish picnic, joining the youth choir, etc.); however, usually participation in the "Give it a Try Stage" begins with a retreat experience. Although one does not necessarily have to begin preparation during the ninth grade, this model calls for a freshman retreat process to begin preferably in the fall or early winter. The Rite of Entrance (Zanzig) is celebrated during the closing liturgy of the retreat (preferably at a parish Mass). It marks the candidates' individual as well as communal openness to continue to be formed in the Way of Christ by their parents and godparents with the help and support of the parish community. Opportunities to experience all eight components of youth ministry are clearly communicated and offered to the candidates and their families throughout this period.

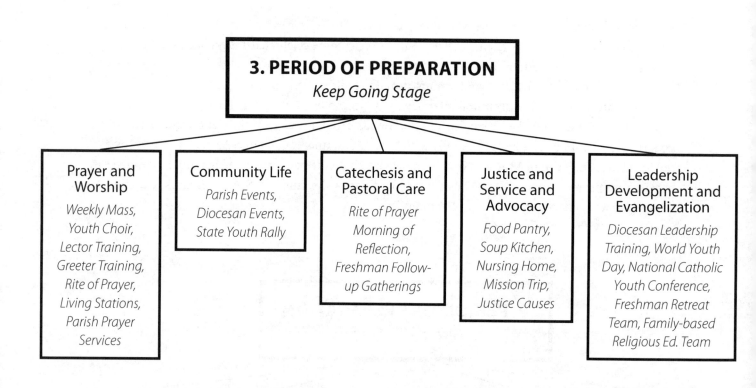

As they move into the "Keep Going Stage," the Rite of Prayer is celebrated by the community as a way to encourage the young people and their parents to deepen their prayer life within the parish. The curriculum remains "the life of the parish." Therefore, a myriad of opportunities within all eight components are offered during this stage. The "Keep Going Stage" typically begins two thirds of the way through freshman year and continues through the first few months of sophomore year.

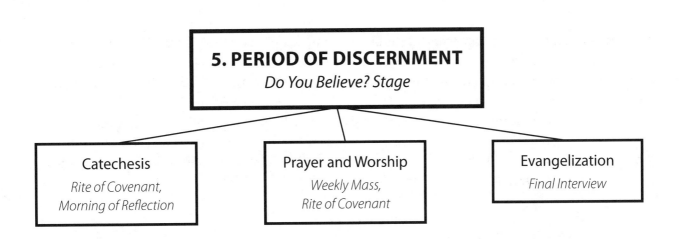

4. PERIOD OF PREPARATION
Get Serious Stage

Prayer and Worship
Weekly Mass, Youth Choir, Lector Training, Greeter Training, Rite of Creed, Living Stations, Parish Prayer Services

Community Life
Parish Events, Diocesan Events, State Youth Rally

Catechesis and Pastoral Care
Rite of Creed Morning of Reflection, Sophomore Retreat, Sophomore Follow-up Gatherings

Justice and Service and Advocacy
Food Pantry, Soup Kitchen, Nursing Home, Mission Trip, Justice Causes

Leadership Development and Evangelization
Diocesan Leadership Training, World Youth Day, National Catholic Youth Conference, Freshman Retreat Team, Family-based Religious Ed. Team

They are called to move into the "Get Serious Stage" during their second year of preparation. This stage begins with the Rite of Creed which allows the parish to invite and challenge the young people to take ownership of the tenets of our faith. A full weekend sophomore retreat experience and weekly follow-up is offered as a vital means through which the candidates can begin to take ownership. (The whole period of preparation can be condensed into one year for parishes whose candidates celebrate confirmation as ninth graders.)

5. PERIOD OF DISCERNMENT
Do You Believe? Stage

Catechesis
Rite of Covenant, Morning of Reflection

Prayer and Worship
Weekly Mass, Rite of Covenant

Evangelization
Final Interview

Once the candidates have had ample opportunities to understand and experience the Christian faith, they may be ready to move into the immediate preparation for confirmation. During this period, the young people are called upon to discern whether or not they wish to choose for themselves to live the rest of their lives in the way of Christ (in other words, do they wish to confirm through the sacrament of confirmation the baptismal promise that their parents and godparents made for them?). This of course requires acceptance of the Roman Catholic religious tradition as their way of expressing their owned Christianity. The Rite of Covenant (Zanzig) marks the beginning of this stage. A final "one-on-one" interview is scheduled with the pastor, youth minister, another pastoral staff member, or catechist (all of whom represent the whole parish community) in order to help each candidate discern (Appendix D). If the candidate discerns "readiness," he or she is then called to spend time thinking about what gifts he or she will share with the parish community after the sacrament is celebrated. Should the candidate with the help of parents and parish discern that he or she is not ready, participation in youth ministry simply continues for that person on an age-appropriate level (even if that participation is with already confirmed peers) until "readiness" is determined. Because pastoral sensitivity is extremely important, the decision to not be confirmed should not mark the end of one's participation in the parish, nor should it be frowned upon. In fact, it should be respected and sometimes commended.

This is a rather brief period. It includes the rite of confirmation, the reflection/rehearsal for the rite, and the reception/parties that follow. Even though the period is brief, we cannot downplay the importance of the sacrament. If it is celebrated authentically, it can be a very powerful and defining event in one's life. (More is said about the rite and the reflection/rehearsal later in this book.) Sponsors are given special attention during this period since they are the ones who commit to directly and consistently supporting the newly confirmed on their faith journey wherever it may take them. (Again, note that the period of celebration does not necessarily have to occur during one's sophomore or junior year of high school. It occurs when one is sincerely ready to celebrate an owned faith.)

7. PERIOD OF MYSTAGOGIA
Time and Talent Stage

Prayer and Worship

Weekly Mass, Youth Choir, Lector Training, Greeter Training, Rite of Creed, Living Stations, Parish Prayer Services

Community Life

Parish Events, Diocesan Events, State Youth Rally

Catechesis and Pastoral Care

Junior and Senior Retreat, Retreat Follow-up Gatherings

Justice and Service and Advocacy

Food Pantry, Soup Kitchen, Nursing Home, Mission Trip, Justice Causes

Leadership Development and Evangelization

Diocesan Leadership Training, World Youth Day, National Catholic Youth Conference, Freshman Retreat Team, Sophomore Retreat Team, Junior/ Senior Retreat Team, Family-based Religious Ed. Team

The neophytes have already discerned what gifts they have to share with the parish community. Now they are invited and encouraged to share those gifts. Some will have many gifts and will share them in various ways. Others may have only one gift to share, such as becoming a certified extraordinary minister of communion or joining a retreat team, but at the very least, all need to understand and be supported in the reality that sharing the gift of themselves at weekly Eucharist is the primary way to live out their confirmation. Since faith formation does not stop at confirmation, a full weekend junior and senior retreat experience and weekly follow-up is offered during this stage. The retreat and follow-up should begin to place more emphasis on Roman Catholicism as a topic of discussion and catechesis. Overall, the period of mystagogia can be likened to one's rookie season in the Major Leagues: You've made it to the show, but you're still a rookie, and you have a lot more to learn! As the graphic on page 42 suggests, the journey is constantly revealing more of the mystery of God.

Four Years of Senior High Youth Ministry with Post-Confirmation

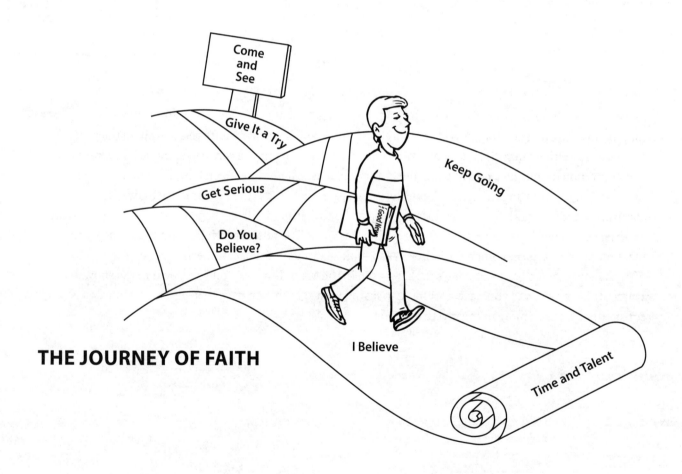

THE JOURNEY OF FAITH

```
┌─────────────────────────────────┐
│     1. COME AND SEE STAGE       │
└─────────────────────────────────┘
                ▼
┌─────────────────────────────────┐
│     2. GIVE IT A TRY STAGE      │
└─────────────────────────────────┘
                ▼
┌─────────────────────────────────┐
│      3. KEEP GOING STAGE        │
└─────────────────────────────────┘
                ▼
┌─────────────────────────────────┐
│      4. GET SERIOUS STAGE       │
└─────────────────────────────────┘
                ▼
┌─────────────────────────────────┐
│     5. DO YOU BELIEVE? STAGE    │
└─────────────────────────────────┘
                ▼
┌─────────────────────────────────┐
│       6. I BELIEVE STAGE        │
└─────────────────────────────────┘
                ▼
┌─────────────────────────────────┐
│    7. TIME AND TALENT STAGE     │
└─────────────────────────────────┘
```

As stated earlier, a post-confirmation senior high youth ministry structure based on initiation theology is essentially the same as if confirmation were celebrated during late adolescence. The stages of faith development do not change; therefore, we have kept the terminology for the seven stages but have dropped the "periods" since these particular young people are already living out their confirmation. Please refer back to the previous pages for a description of each stage. The following descriptions will only point out the differences that occur with a post-confirmation youth ministry.

Instead of a Rite of Welcome, a ritual blessing occurs within a regular parish liturgy early in the fall. At some point during the freshmen/parent gathering that follows the liturgy, the freshmen will be asked to schedule a "get to know you" interview with one of the catechists present (see Appendix E).

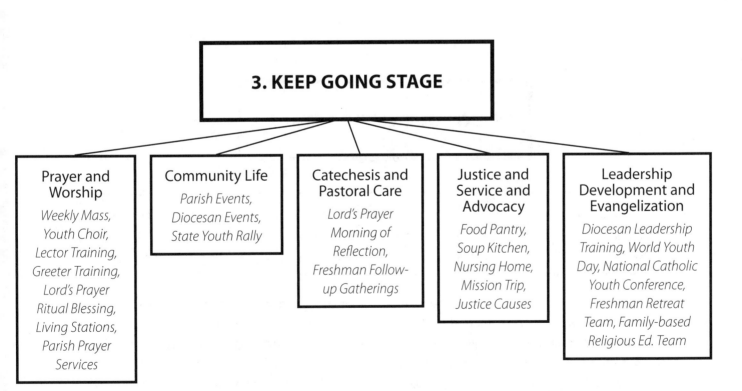

2. GIVE IT A TRY STAGE

Prayer and Worship

Weekly Mass, Youth Choir, Lector Training, Greeter Training, Entrance Ritual Blessing, Living Stations, Parish Prayer Services

Community Life

Parish Events, Diocesan Events, State Youth Rally

Catechesis and Pastoral Care

Freshman Retreat, Freshman Follow-up Gatherings

Justice and Service and Advocacy

Food Pantry, Soup Kitchen, Nursing Home, Mission Trip, Justice Causes

Leadership Development and Evangelization

Diocesan Leadership Training, World Youth Day, National Catholic Youth Conference

Instead of a Rite of Entrance, a ritual blessing is incorporated into the closing liturgy for the freshman retreat. The ritual blessing is an opportunity for the freshmen to acknowledge that they are willing to participate in all eight components of youth ministry as a means through which they may arrive at an owned faith.

3. KEEP GOING STAGE

Prayer and Worship

Weekly Mass, Youth Choir, Lector Training, Greeter Training, Lord's Prayer Ritual Blessing, Living Stations, Parish Prayer Services

Community Life

Parish Events, Diocesan Events, State Youth Rally

Catechesis and Pastoral Care

Lord's Prayer Morning of Reflection, Freshman Follow-up Gatherings

Justice and Service and Advocacy

Food Pantry, Soup Kitchen, Nursing Home, Mission Trip, Justice Causes

Leadership Development and Evangelization

Diocesan Leadership Training, World Youth Day, National Catholic Youth Conference, Freshman Retreat Team, Family-based Religious Ed. Team

The Rite of Prayer in the previous model becomes a ritual blessing in this model. It is preceded by the same family-based "morning of reflection."

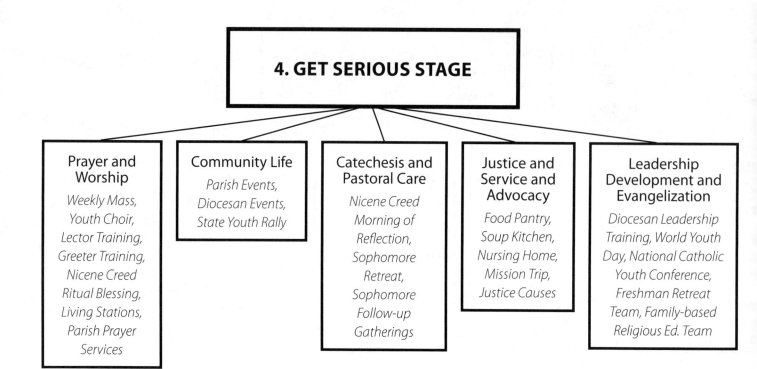

4. GET SERIOUS STAGE

Prayer and Worship
Weekly Mass, Youth Choir, Lector Training, Greeter Training, Nicene Creed Ritual Blessing, Living Stations, Parish Prayer Services

Community Life
Parish Events, Diocesan Events, State Youth Rally

Catechesis and Pastoral Care
Nicene Creed Morning of Reflection, Sophomore Retreat, Sophomore Follow-up Gatherings

Justice and Service and Advocacy
Food Pantry, Soup Kitchen, Nursing Home, Mission Trip, Justice Causes

Leadership Development and Evangelization
Diocesan Leadership Training, World Youth Day, National Catholic Youth Conference, Freshman Retreat Team, Family-based Religious Ed. Team

One thing to note here: The Rite of Creed in the former model is a ritual blessing around the profession of faith in this model. It is preceded by a family-based morning of reflection that uses the same template as the Rite of Creed.

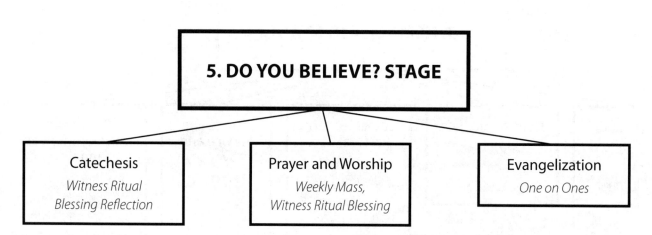

5. DO YOU BELIEVE? STAGE

Catechesis
Witness Ritual Blessing Reflection

Prayer and Worship
Weekly Mass, Witness Ritual Blessing

Evangelization
One on Ones

Since the Rite of Covenant is so closely related to the sacrament of confirmation, creating a similar ritual blessing and morning of reflection for post-confirmation sophomores/juniors/seniors does not make much pastoral sense. Instead, as a way to provide the young people with an opportunity to acknowledge that they have had an encounter with Jesus and are willing to take some time to think about where they are in their faith development, a witness ritual blessing is incorporated into the parish Masses during the lenten season. After the homily, the candidates are encouraged to give a public witness as to where they are in their faith. A family-based reflection helps prepare the young people for the ritual blessing. Also in this stage, during the course of the next few or many months, the sophomores/juniors/seniors are invited by their youth minister or catechists or priests to have a sit-down, open and honest "one-on-one" conversation about the current state of their faith. There is no timetable. In fact, it is possible for one to remain in the "Do You Believe Stage" right through senior year and even into college (but hopefully no longer than that). Whatever the case, it is important that the young people choose for themselves to give witness. Of course, age-appropriate participation in all eight components of youth ministry continues on through this stage, should one decide to delay the next stage.

Since the young people have now reached the stage in their faith development where they fully understand (primarily through experience and relationship) what a Christian lifestyle is, they are now invited to wholeheartedly and publicly declare their intention to live that lifestyle as a result of their own choice (in addition to the choice that their parents made for them). In preparation for a ritual blessing that expresses this declaration, a retreat or day of renewal may take place with or without parents. Perhaps even a dinner reception could follow as a way to enhance the celebratory nature of the event.

7. TIME AND TALENT STAGE

Prayer and Worship
Weekly Mass, Youth Choir, Lector Training, Greeter Training, Rite of Creed, Living Stations, Parish Prayer Services

Community Life
Parish Events, Diocesan Events, State Youth Rally

Catechesis and Pastoral Care
Junior and Senior Retreat, Retreat Follow-up Gatherings

Justice and Service and Advocacy
Food Pantry, Soup Kitchen, Nursing Home, Mission Trip, Justice Causes

Leadership Development and Evangelization
Diocesan Leadership Training, World Youth Day, National Catholic Youth Conference, Freshman Retreat Team, Sophomore Retreat Team, Junior/ Senior Retreat Team, Family-based Religious Ed. Team

It is simply assumed that anyone who has ritually and publicly declared his or her intention to embrace Christianity through the Roman Catholic tradition will actively seek out opportunities to share his/her time and talent with the parish community. As always, an initiation-based youth ministry offers a plethora of opportunities at this stage and beyond.

Overall, the different stages of senior high youth ministry follow a progression. The beginning year(s) are like an "internship." Through baptism, we became a part of the Church, but we still have more to experience before we are asked to fully take ownership of our Christian discipleship. The parish in essence asks its young people to give all eight components of youth ministry a try so that they can know what a person with an owned faith is supposed to be like (someone who serves others, worships and prays, shares one's faith with all generations, etc.). We can then base our decision to be or not to be confirmed or to declare or not declare an owned faith on sufficient experience. Once we do confirm the reality of an owned faith, we are called to continue to live out our baptism through the life of the parish and the liturgical year as our expression of committed belonging.

By taking this approach to senior high youth ministry, we are being more consistent not only with the U.S. Bishops' vision, but with the early Church as well. Christian initiation in the early Church was a commitment to the mission and ministry of Jesus Christ as lived out in the community. By allowing young people to move through the different stages at their own pace, and by placing the emphasis on conversion as opposed to "requirements," we most effectively reach the goals of total youth ministry. This is how a parish can deepen its call to young people, empowering them to come forward and take ownership of their faith.

SECTION FOUR

AGE-APPROPRIATE AND INTERGENERATIONAL OPPORTUNITIES

Has a young person in your parish ever said, "Thank you for the opportunity" or said something similar? If not, you have a serious problem. The main function of youth ministry is to provide opportunities primarily for but not limited to youth and their families so that they may live out their baptismal call. As much as it is good and right that we in parish leadership thank our catechists, volunteers, and peer leaders for giving their time and talent, they should just as much thank *us* for giving *them* the opportunity. That's what a parish structure does. It provides a Catholic community with a place and venue through which to live out their faith.

But often times, we in parish leadership do not support this notion with the verbiage that we use. For example, I know a priest who at the end of every Mass says, "Thank you for coming." As nice as that is to hear, we can easily misunderstand such a comment and conclude that we did that priest a favor by showing up to celebrate Eucharist. I know that when I am thanked for showing up at something, the message sent to me is that my presence and participation is not an opportunity for me, but a gesture for someone else. This kind of "favor language" is often used more than "opportunity language" among parish leaders.

In fact, let's be honest. Many parish leaders do not use opportunity language at all. Parish leadership can often view its role as those who are responsible for recruiting volunteers to ministry as opposed to those responsible for empowering ministers. DREs and youth ministers in particular tend to be most guilty of this. We find ourselves in recruiting mode, especially as start-up dates creep closer and closer, and we still need more people. Eventually desperation sets in, and we begin to ask people to "do me a favor." Worse yet, we resort to begging people, groveling for their time, even if they have no talent. We become satisfied with "any warm body" to teach that seventh grade religious class or to teach that ninth grade confirmation class. The result (more often than not) is parishioners volunteering to do things in ministry

not so much as an opportunity for themselves, but as a favor to us; therefore the quality is not what it could be. Keep in mind that this whole scenario often occurs within a ministry structure that the DRE and/or youth minister themselves put in place! (Remember the Einstein quote about the definition of insanity: Doing the same thing over and over again and expecting different results.)

A BAPTISMAL CALL

Parish priests, religious and lay ministers should never say to a parishioner: "Could you do me a favor and do this?" Participation in ministry is about answering a baptismal call, not answering a phone call.

Don't get me wrong. I do not mean that personal invitation is bad. Personal invitation is usually how most people begin their participation in ministry. What I mean is that personal invitation should use opportunity language and not favor language. For example: "Joe, I do not know if you realize this, but you have a lot of enthusiasm and a great voice. You would bring a lot of life to our youth choir. What do you think?" Here Joe is invited to use his gift as an opportunity to bring life. If he says, "yes," he will begin this ministry with a positive and self-giving attitude. He will be motivated by the prospect that his gifts can be used to make a difference.

Renewing the Vision describes how youth ministry is an opportunity and how this opportunity should, as often as possible, be age-appropriate and intergenerational.

> Effective ministry with adolescents provides developmentally appropriate experiences, programs, activities, strategies, resources, content, and processes to address the unique developmental and social needs of young and older adolescents both as individuals and as members of families. (p. 20)

> Ministry with adolescents can incorporate young people into the intergenerational

opportunities already available in the parish community, identify and develop leadership opportunities in the parish for young people, and create intergenerational support networks and mentoring relationships. (p. 22)

At first glance, the terms "age-appropriate" and "intergenerational" seem to be at odds. If something is designed for a specific age group, how can it be intergenerational? The simple answer is: sometimes it can, sometimes it can't. The important thing is that young people in our parishes have the opportunity to experience both, either simultaneously or separately. Both are key elements in the ongoing faith formation of young people.

In this section, we will examine the major ways in which a senior high youth ministry can provide age-appropriate and intergenerational opportunities.

Youth-Friendly Masses

I frequently tell the story of the "best Mass I have ever experienced." It was the farewell Mass for the retiring pastor of my home parish. As I tell the story, I am quick to point out that I don't remember what the songs were and whether or not I liked them. I don't remember what the readings were nor do I remember the homily and whether or not it was a good one. I can't remember if the Mass lasted longer or shorter than one hour, and I don't even remember who was sitting next to me. The only thing I remember about that Mass is that everyone in the church participated fully, consciously, and actively. There was not a person in the house (from my perspective) who did not sing, who did not pray, who did not listen, and who did not come to put their whole self on the altar. I can honestly say that no other time or event in my life before or after that Mass has the Holy Spirit ever been more recognizable to me (and I've been to numerous World Youth Days, to the top of mountain peaks, on countless retreats, to St. Peter's Basilica for Mass, etc.). All it took was an authentically worshipping community to make the real presence of Jesus recognizable. Another thing that I remember from after that experience was thinking to myself: "I can't wait to do this again!"

That is when I finally understood what we mean when we say "Sunday obligation." For most of my life that phrase conjured negative images. It portrayed an image of Mass as something that we have to do on Sunday whether we like it or not, so we might as well go and get it over with. Although it is true that our Church teaches that Mass is an obligation, the teaching was never meant to convey the negative connotation that prevails with most Catholics.

For example, my brother is a die-hard Yankee fan, where as I find baseball rather boring and slow. If my brother were to get Yankee tickets to the World Series, he would say with excitement, "I have to go!" If he needed someone last minute to go with him, I might say begrudgingly, "I guess I have to go." My brother's obligation is out of desire to be with his team. My obligation is out of the guilt that I would have if I didn't go with him.

A POSITIVE ATTITUDE

Our Sunday obligation is meant to be understood as an attitude that says, "I have to go to Mass to be with my God and my community!" It is not meant to be a guilt-ridden attitude that begrudgingly says, "I guess I have to go to Mass."

From my experience, the majority of Catholic youth tend to have this second attitude. "Why do we have to go to Mass?" is the question that almost every Catholic young person asks at some point in his or her life. This question is usually followed by a number of frustrated statements and more questions. This then prompts parents to approach their parish leadership pleading for more youth-friendly Masses.

So how do we make our Masses more youth-friendly? I believe that the starting point is promoting full, conscious, and active participation among *all* the faithful during our Eucharistic celebrations. There is no better way for a community to form the faith of its young and old than through good liturgy.

This then begs the question: How do we do this? How do parishes not only get all their parishioners to come to Mass, but to fully participate once they are there? How do we get them to say, "I can't wait to do this again!" I do not contend that I have figured out what seemingly no one else (not even the pope) has figured out, but I do have a suggestion that, to my knowledge, no parish has tried.

Many American parishes have gone through, are going through, or are planning to go through what has become known as a "capital campaign." Extra money is needed for new buildings and/or renovations of old buildings. This involves committees of parishioners and staff, parish-wide mailings, appeals from the pulpit, phone calls, meetings, pledges, and visits to parishioners' homes all for one purpose: money. The pastor in particular does a lot of running around from one home to another asking for donations that in the end will help "enhance the spiritual life of the parish."

Imagine for a moment if a parish decided to put this same kind of time, energy, and personnel behind a "Mass-participation campaign." Imagine the same amount of mailings and phone calls and committee meetings and appeals from the pulpit and home visits. Imagine the pastor going from home to home asking parishioners to make a pledge to participate fully, consciously, and actively at Sunday Mass that will in the end help "enhance the spiritual life of the parish."

GOOD LITURGY FOR YOUTH

The point of this suggestion is that good liturgy for the whole parish is good liturgy for youth. When the whole parish participates, Jesus is truly re-membered (his real presence is brought back) and recognized within the worshipping community. There is nothing better a parish can do that will make Mass more youth-friendly than by focusing a huge amount of time and energy on building good liturgy. "If you build it, they will come!"

This is why a "youth Mass" is not really the long-term answer to having more youth-friendly Masses. The concept of a "youth Mass" severely damages the vision of an intergenerational parish. It gathers primarily only one generation for Eucharist and therefore fails to represent the larger community. It drives a wedge between the youth and the rest of the parish. What is conveyed is that youth are separate from the rest of the community: they have their own Mass, with their own priest, their own music, and their own liturgical ministers. Youth Masses may seem like a good idea to a parish that is struggling to get youth involved, especially when we see other parishes attracting many, many young people with their youth Mass; but in the long run, they may not be fostering their personal and spiritual growth because of the separation from the total life of the parish (which, as we have learned, is the "curriculum" for youth ministry).

A STRONG YOUTH PRESENCE

Instead of having youth Mass, a parish could have a regular Sunday liturgy that simply acknowledges a strong youth presence. It's a subtle difference in semantics, but a huge difference in message. Suggestion: Pick a regular parish liturgy and make a concerted and deliberate effort to incorporate youth on a weekly basis. Perhaps put youth representatives on the liturgy committee to ensure that this happens. If young people are properly trained as lectors, greeters, and ministers of communion, schedule them alongside adults at that Mass. If youth are not liturgical ministers, provide ongoing training for them to become liturgical ministers. If you have a youth ministry sponsored choir/band (preferably consisting of youth and adults) and/or cantors, schedule them at that Mass. Maybe once or twice a year a young person can deliver a prepared witness talk based on the day's readings before the homily.

The celebration of Eucharist is without a doubt the greatest opportunity that we all have to live out our faith. When Mass is done well and all participate fully, consciously, and actively, our youth will follow suit. Also, when young people are given the opportunity to celebrate Eucharist with the larger community and in a way that utilizes their gifts, we are doing nothing short of making them active members of the community. *Lex orandi, lex credendi* (worship forms faith).

Retreat Processes

Almost every parish understands that retreats are important and must be used within their youth ministry. An initiation model, however, recognizes retreat processes as not only important, but as vital to adolescent faith formation. Please note that I refer to retreat processes and not simply retreats.

This model calls for a process that begins with establishing a team of confirmed youth who are empowered to direct the retreat for their peers as well as facilitate weekly follow-up gatherings. The retreat itself is just one part of the entire process, albeit a very important part. This model also calls for a process that is to take place within the parish community (on parish grounds with parishioner support). Lastly, there should be at least three different and developmentally appropriate retreat processes within a senior high youth ministry, one for freshmen, one for sophomores, and at least one for juniors and seniors.

Here is the rationale for making retreat processes central and some practical suggestions on how to make them more effective.

Vital to Adolescent Faith Formation Nothing in my experience in youth ministry has had a more profound effect than a good retreat experience. I have seen good retreat processes not only affect candidates but catechists, peer leaders, parents, and regular parishioners as well. Why not take the success of a good retreat and use it as a springboard for effective catechesis and motivated participation in parish? This is one of the other reasons why we at my home parish gave up on monthly confirmation sessions. Young people were voluntarily coming to weekly retreat follow-up gatherings with enthusiasm and spirit. The same kids were coming to confirmation sessions out of negative obligation and with an attitude. It simply made a lot of sense to replace the confirmation sessions with retreat follow-up gatherings. We were essentially giving them the same lectionary-based catechesis, only this time in an environment that they wanted to be in because of the great experience they had on the retreat. Sound too good to be true? Well, it just might be because all of this depends on whether or not the retreat experience is a positive one. In my experience, there are two major factors that ensure a good retreat: time and detail. An enormous commitment of time is needed by many people who are willing to pay close attention to detail. A good retreat depends on a committed and detail-oriented team who are willing to make their involvement in this ministry a priority in their lives.

Formation of a Team A parish could bring in an outside team to direct their retreat, as many do; however, if a parish youth ministry is to use an initiation model, it is the parish community that must take on this responsibility. Outside groups may run a fine retreat, but they offer no ongoing follow-up. The leadership that is offered lasts only as long as the retreat itself. When a team of young parishioners is formed with guidance from adult catechists, the parish is not only providing peer leadership but is empowering its confirmed upperclasses and adult catechists to share their faith on an ongoing basis.

It creates a cycle where catechists share faith with team leaders in order to show them how to share faith with their younger peers. The younger adolescents learn how to share faith through the retreat process experience and hopefully become future leaders. The team leaders witness the joy of being an adult catechist through the relational ministry that takes place on the team and hopefully become young adult catechists themselves later in life (maybe even ecclesial, religious, or ordained ministers). Adult catechists in this model actually spend more time ministering to and with the team leaders than they do with the younger candidates. Again, the developmental reality is that older adolescents (eleventh and twelfth graders) are much more ready to form solid faith-based relationships with adults than are their younger peers. Therefore, the intergenerational mentorship that is called for by *Renewing the Vision* is realized more effectively when adult parishioners mentor older adolescents who in turn mentor younger adolescents.

This is not to say that younger adolescents are not afforded the opportunity to share faith with adult catechists within this model. They certainly do, albeit in an age-appropriate and non-intimidating way. However, it must be understood that the upperclass team has a much greater chance of influencing an authentic conversion experience with younger adolescents than do adult catechists. This is why putting together and empowering a team is crucial. First, it is wise to empower two or three leaders who serve as the leaders of the team. These should be seniors who have been on a retreat team in the past and have shown excellent organizational skills and have been active parishioners.

The first of many jobs for these "team directors" is to personally invite others to be on the team (using opportunity language). Of course, the team is not just picked on a whim. Careful consideration for potential team leaders will have already been done by the adult coordinator and catechists before personal invitations are made. Once the team is formed, each team leader is assigned a witness talk on some topic (depending on which retreat model one is using). The team leaders are also trained in basic listening skills and small and large group leadership. (See Appendix E.)

Team Meetings The youth directors on the team should meet for at least thirty minutes with the adult coordinator(s) before each team meeting in order to go over the night's agenda that they themselves will implement. A typical team meeting agenda will include an opening prayer, icebreaker (if necessary), time to hear and critique each other's witness talk drafts, time to practice small group leadership skills, time to sing, break time, announcements, and closing prayer. Example: Jack and Diane are both seniors and are the co-directors for the Shmang Retreat process. They show up at the youth ministry center at 6:15 PM on a Sunday night to meet with you, the youth minister, in order to go over the 7 PM Shmang Retreat Team *Meeting agenda*. Jack is responsible for the opening prayer, so as usual, the three of you listen to the Word of the day's gospel proclaimed once again. You ask Jack and Diane what words or phases stuck out in their minds and gradually use those themes to help Jack formulate the words to the opening prayer that he will later lead. Then, the three of you come to a consensus on a good reflection question based on the lectionary theme of the day's gospel that Diane will present to the team. The other parts of the agenda all fall into place, and you are ready.

Jack and Diane greet the team and adult catechists as they arrive at 6:55 PM (arriving early so as to begin on time). Jack calls everyone to prayer at 7 PM, inviting all to hold hands. His words lead all in prayer, and he concludes with an intercessory prayer (in his own words) through Mary and finally invites all to join him in praying the Hail Mary.

Diane reminds everyone that rough drafts are due today. As a quick icebreaker, she invites the team to rate their week from 1-10 (1 being the worst week of their life, 10 being the best week ever). She sits them in a horseshoe in ascending order and everyone shares (including the adults).

After the icebreaker, she divides the team into four small groups, each with at least one adult, to go over talks. She reminds everyone before they break that good feedback requires that they listen carefully to what each other has written and then share what they liked, what they found confusing, what they think is too much, too little, too preachy, etc. (Witness talk critique should be based on the hand-out that they would have received at an earlier meeting. See Appendix F. Later meetings should have critique of talk delivery instead of talk content. See Appendix G for the handout.) All break into groups and return forty minutes later for a ten-minute snack break.

After the break, Jack hands out song books and organizes everyone into a circle. He reminds everyone that we will be encouraging the candidates to sing on the retreat and therefore need to practice ourselves. A couple of team leaders whip out their guitars and lead everyone in some popular hymnal songs mixed in with some positive secular songs.

After twenty minutes of singing, Diane regains some calmness among the team before she stands and proclaims the gospel (from Mass earlier in the day). Then she offers the reflection question with the instruction that all are to go back into their groups and pick a leader who is to lead a discussion using the gospel and reflection question as a starter. Diane also reminds everyone to end the discussion at a certain time in order to have time to give feedback on the strengths and weaknesses of the leader's small group leadership skills (based on Appendix E, which would have been handed out and explained at an earlier meeting).

When the group comes back together, Jack goes over the announcements which include some service opportunities that are coming up, a reminder that the team will go together to the 12:00 Mass next Sunday and get some lunch afterwards, and that typed copies of their rough drafts are due next week. After answering some questions, Diane lights a candle, calls everyone back to prayer, invites all to share out loud any petition to God that they have, and concludes with the Lord's Prayer.

Within the Parish Community In my experience and through my research of senior high retreat processes, the model that I think has the best philosophy is the *New Antioch Retreat* by Jerry and Mary Mandry, which is an adaptation of a University of Notre Dame retreat by a small parish in Dobbs Ferry, New York, beginning in the late 1970s. I believe this because the Antioch philosophy is totally parish-based. As the U.S. bishops state:

> The parish is where the Church lives. Parishes are communities of faith, of action, and of hope. They are where the Gospel is proclaimed and celebrated, where believers are formed and sent to renew the earth. Parishes are the home of the Christian community; they are the heart of our Church. Parishes are the place where God's people meet Jesus in Word and sacrament and come in touch with the source of the Church's life. (*Communities of Salt and Light*, p. 1)

It is extremely difficult to give young people a sense that their parish is "home" when we send them away on retreat. It is also just as difficult to encourage adult parishioners to consider its youth full members of the parish when they are seldom given opportunities to get to know them and support them. *The New Antioch Manual* expands this philosophy:

> Special effort is needed to bring the youth into regular contact with the whole parish. If teenagers become a satellite community, connected to the broader Church in name only, they fail to benefit from the nurturing of a worshipping, witnessing community of faith. (p.3)

The New Antioch model recognizes that "retreat" for a young person does not necessarily have to mean "away." After all, what is the point of a youth retreat? Is it not a retreat from what society would have us believe is most important in life (school, sports, our own circle of friends, television, cell phones, etc.)?

A good retreat experience asks its candidates to focus on three things and only three things: God, oneself, and the community. What makes Antioch so prophetic is that it recognizes what all other retreat models at the time of its inception failed to recognize: what young people really need is a faith experience that not only connects them to each other, but to the parish community as well.

A SPACE ON PARISH GROUNDS

And so a parish-based retreat process requires a space on parish grounds for the team to meet on a weekly basis, lots of space on parish grounds for the weekend retreat experience, and space for the weekly follow-up gatherings. The church building should also be available for certain prayer services and, of course, Eucharist. We already know that the team consists of young parishioners and adult catechists, but other parishioners can be involved as well. Families and individuals from the parish can cook and serve meals, serve as host home families, and be asked to pray for those on retreat.

The host home experience especially makes a huge difference. To quote *The New Antioch Manual*:

> In order to sustain the spirit and momentum of the weekend process, careful attention is given to the period of time during which teenagers are assigned to sleep groups in the homes of parishioners....The hospitality extended by the host family creates a sense of security and comfort which is essential. This type of housing arrangement also provides an opportunity for teen and adult members of a parish to meet in a new and different way.

Upperclass team leaders continue the process of the retreat by accompanying three or four retreat candidates to the host home to facilitate a discussion and prayer before turning in for the night (of course, no gender mixing). When the two disciples at Emmaus recognized Jesus and he vanished from their sight, it wasn't the Lord Jesus who vanished, but the stranger! The host home experience allows our youth to share themselves with one another and the host family in the way one shares bread with friends. It makes the stranger in each other disappear!

During the past twenty-five years, thousands of youth and adults have gone through this experience in my home parish and have witnessed firsthand the hospitality and trust that has taken place. They have learned more about "being parish" from that experience than they will ever learn from a homily or a textbook. Sadly, many dioceses have decided to discontinue host homes as a response to the recent sexual abuse scandals in the Church. (I obviously believe that such a decision, although well intentioned, is a bad one.) Overall, the parish-based model for retreat processes is more consistent with initiation theology than any other model and therefore makes a huge difference within a parish youth ministry.

Follow-up Gatherings This is what makes a retreat process truly a process. After a good retreat experience, there is usually a great deal of excitement and enthusiasm within the candidates and team. Follow-up gatherings allow the young people to keep alive the Spirit that enflamed them on the retreat. Follow-up gatherings prevent the retreat from being a "one-shot deal" or just a nice memory by affording the candidates and team the opportunity to reunite on a weekly basis.

Follow-ups also help ease the candidates back into the real world because in all frankness, what a person experiences on a retreat is not at all what the real world is like. In the real world, people do not always accept you unconditionally and want to know what you think. In the real world, it is not socially acceptable to talk about one's faith. There is no "singing time" in the real world of a teenager, nor are there daily affirmation letters. There are no hours of silent reflection/prayer, no elaborately decorated name-tags, no endless pounds of baked ziti, and no upperclassers who seem really excited to see you. A good retreat experience does for the young people what the Transfiguration did for Peter, James, and John: provides a glimpse of heaven. But just as the apostles had to go down the mountain and back into the world, so must the candidates and team. And just as the apostles went back into the world changed, so do the young people.

The question is now, how will *they* change the world? Follow-ups essentially deal with this question and others like it: how do we make our communities more like the one we formed on the retreat? What is it about the real world that makes it difficult to be a Christian? Are there people in our lives that we should treat differently now that we have experienced this retreat? And the discussion continues week after week. But be careful. The follow-up experience can easily become a weekly mini-retreat or place for the young people to retreat from the real world. A follow-up gathering should be just the opposite: a chance to support each other in making the real world better. This is done by breaking open the Word and discussing how to apply the weekly gospel message to everyday life.

Lectionary-based Catechesis As mentioned earlier in this book, the primary source that is used in this model of youth ministry, especially at follow-up gatherings is the Word of God, or more specifically, the lectionary readings. All eight components of youth ministry flow out of Mass as much as possible, especially catechesis. Just as adult catechumens and candidates break open the Word as a starting point for their catechesis, so too do the youth. There have been many differing points of view over recent years concerning the use of lectionary-based catechesis, especially with children and youth. There are those who seem to be convinced that lectionary-based catechesis is wrong, and there are those, like me, who are convinced that it is right, at least when applied appropriately. Like most stubborn people, I believe that I can convince even the nay-sayers to come on board. Here is the argument for lectionary-based catechesis within youth ministry:

1. *Eucharist is the source of all ministry, including catechesis.* The Liturgy of the Word is a part of our Eucharist and is therefore a part of the source of all ministry within the Church. Lectionary-based catechesis reminds me of a typical family get-together in my house. Coming from an Italian-American family, eating good food is only part of the meal experience for us. Whenever my family has a meal, we always talk about the food after we eat it: the mussels were fantastic; where did you find the recipe for that corn casserole; I haven't had meatballs like that in a long time. Just like in my family's meals, lectionary-based catechesis is the natural progression of the Eucharistic meal: we talk about the food that was fed to us at the Table of the Word. How did it fill us? How is it a part of us now? Just as we share stories and memories around our family table, we share our Christian memory from the table of the lectionary, and we are fed.

2. *All of our tradition is rooted in Sacred Scripture.* Catholic doctrine has come about as a result of centuries of breaking open the Word. We in ministry leadership can very easily get tied down to scheduling catechetical sessions around Catholic doctrine topics because somewhere along the line, we have been convinced that certain topics must be covered by a certain time no matter what. We often use Sacred Scripture to support the doctrine, but in reality, it is the doctrine that supports some aspect of Scripture.

   We allow publishers and authors of textbooks to tell us what topics are to be covered and when they are to be covered. It is easy for us to forget that textbooks should be seen as a supplemental to and not the focus of our catechetical efforts. The lectionary cycle provides for us the story of our salvation and reveals to us who we are and who our God is, and thus should always be the focus. Catholic doctrine can always be presented and taught as the Church's response to the gospel message. This way, young people can see where the teachings come from. Simply put: we read the lectionary, and then the lectionary reads us.

3. *Lectionary-based catechesis supports a Universal Church.* If the rest of the Catholic world is reflecting on a lectionary theme at a given time, so too should our children and youth reflect on the same theme because they are just as much a part of the Church as anyone else. When children and youth are given a curriculum that does not correspond to the lectionary cycle, it is just one more wedge driven between them and what the rest of the Church is experiencing and reflecting upon.

4. *Lectionary-based catechesis is a family-based strategy* and makes being the primary faith giver easier for parents. For instance, when a teenager is leaving for or comes home from a retreat follow-up gathering, the parent already knows the topic (the gospel of the day or previous Sunday) and can open a dialogue. At the very least, simply by attending Mass and paying attention, the parent will always know the curriculum topic of the day. (See Appendix H for an example of a lectionary-based follow-up gathering.)

 # Justice and Service Opportunities

We cannot be called truly "Catholic" unless we hear and heed the Church's call to serve those in need and work for justice and peace. We cannot call ourselves followers of Jesus unless we take up his mission of bringing "good news to the poor, liberty to captives, and new sight to the blind." (*Communities of Salt and Light*, p.3, U.S. bishops)

Imagine if every Catholic in the United States took this statement seriously. Imagine if fifty percent of Catholics in our country took this statement seriously! Heck, imagine if only twenty-five percent of Catholics took this statement seriously!! What a different nation we would have! What a different American Church we would have!

The truth is that most American Catholics do not take this statement seriously. If we did, we would either have a lot of people who no longer call themselves Catholic or we would have much less poverty and injustice. The reality is that even in a post-Vatican II Church, most American Catholics do not identify their catholicity with service to others. They are Catholics because they

were brought up Catholic and received Catholic sacraments, but certainly not because they "hear and heed the Church's call to serve those in need and work for justice and peace." Many Catholics still do not make the connection between Eucharist and service (remember that in John's gospel, the eucharistic narrative is about foot-washing).

As baptized Christians and as Catholics, we believe that our membership in the Body of Christ is defined by how we treat one another. "Amen, I say to you, whatever you did for one of these least brothers and sisters of mine, you did for me" (Matthew 25:40). There is, however, a dangerous misunderstanding that comes with this belief. We refer to this danger as "altruism."

When our outreach is not processed and put into context, we run the risk of losing our eucharistic identity and replacing it with an altruistic identity. Altruism in its purest state is a good thing. It means "unselfish regard for or devotion to the welfare of others." Now how can that be risky? The risk with an altruistic attitude is that it can become impersonal and condescending. Often, our service (or mission work) in the Church can take on this attitude.

For example, I used to think of our parish trips to Appalachia in the summer as a good way to "expose" our youth to "those people" living in poverty. I saw it as an opportunity for us, the wealthy, to serve them, the poor. My attitude was altruistic in the sense that it was selfless and didn't expect anything in return. But I certainly was not thinking of the people that we served as true brothers and sisters and as part of my family. They were separate from my world except for one week in the summer.

Then one day, I was having a conversation with a parent concerning her teen's potential participation in the Appalachia Help Week. I proceeded to say to her, as I had said to many other parents on many other occasions, that the trip is so worthwhile because it teaches us to appreciate what we have. Afterward, it hit me. I imagined saying the same thing to one of the families in West Virginia: "The reason why I am helping you is because when I see how poor you are, it helps me appreciate what I have at home."

RECOGNIZING MY EQUALS

I became so disgusted with myself. I never realized how insulting, impersonal, and condescending I had been for so long. I never truly recognized the people in Appalachia as my equals. They existed so that I and other "knights in shining armor" could help them. If their poverty would have magically disappeared one day, I would have been disappointed that they didn't need help anymore. How warped is that?

Obviously, my attitude has since changed, and I try to see all mission work from a eucharistic perspective. In other words, I serve my brothers and sisters in Appalachia not because they are poor, but because they are my brothers and sisters in the Lord Jesus. Catholic Social Teaching refers to this attitude as "solidarity": we are connected to everyone!

It is no wonder that John and the early Church put so much emphasis on connecting Eucharist to service. Eucharist is not about an impersonal

and condescending attitude of service where the rich "throw the poor a bone" every once in a while. Eucharist is about mutual serving and gift giving/receiving. It's about solidarity. Every time we say "Amen" to the Body and Blood of Christ, we are acknowledging that all humans are our brothers and sisters, that we are all one in Christ. It is through this communion with each other that we find our God. The challenge for our parishes is to take on this attitude of solidarity and then pass it on to our youth.

A LIFESTYLE OF SERVICE

An initiation model once again calls the whole parish community to go back to its earliest roots, back to when being "Catholic" or "Christian" meant living a deliberate lifestyle of loving service. In order to truly be a Catholic Christian, one must serve others and seek justice as a way of life. In a sense, it is a "requirement" for all Catholics, but a requirement that is never fulfilled, never completed. It doesn't end with confirmation because there is always more.

This is why all justice and service opportunities within the parish can and should be shared by all: children, youth, and adults (with age-appropriate exceptions). We cannot teach our young people that being a Catholic Christian means serving others and seeking justice when the rest of the parish community does not serve others or seek justice on a regular basis.

So once again, the way to do a certain aspect of youth ministry that works depends on the vision of the parish community. If there is an overall emphasis on outreach in the parish with ample opportunities to serve, the youth can plug right in with the rest of the community. That's right! My experience in youth ministry has convinced me that young people should not be presented with "their own" justice and service opportunities. They should be encouraged to participate in the total parish's outreach opportunities with other parishioners, young and old, by right of baptism. Whether or not someone is confirmed should make no difference. The expectation of *all* parishioners is that they "heed the Church's call to serve those in need and work for justice and peace." This is a strong belief that can only be instilled in young people by the example of their parents and parish community.

PARISHWIDE OUTREACH

So how do we do the component of justice and service within this model? The first step is working with the pastor and other parish leaders in creating a parish outreach ministry, preferably with a paid staff coordinator. The second step involves coordinating and communicating the ongoing service opportunities and justice-seeking efforts for and to the whole parish throughout the year. The third step is to make a sign-up board and/or web site sign-up easily accessible to all parishioners (perhaps a large outreach sign-up area in the narthex of the church). The last step is to make sure that the communication of these opportunities to youth and their families is reinforced and reiterated through youth ministry (mailings, emails, sign-ups at mornings of reflection, follow-up gatherings, etc.).

This then begs the question: what kind of opportunities should be provided by the parish? It would be a mistake for a parish to choose certain service opportunities or justice causes simply to keep its parishioners busy or to provide a variety. Whatever a parish's outreach effort is, it should be based on the needs of the surrounding community and the needs of other communities asking for help concerning the injustice that affects them. In other words, we do not do service just for the sake of doing service. There always needs to be a connection with and a sincere care for those whom we serve.

We must ask ourselves what the point is of serving others and seeking justice. Ultimately, we believe that through Eucharist, it is our mission to go out into the world and be the Body of Christ for one another. We are all missionaries, assigned to be the Body of Christ to those around us. It's a team effort. No one person is asked to save the world. We each minister to a certain "territory," so to speak, and together see that the whole world is covered. That's the point: to continue the mission of Jesus as a communal effort. This means that we must put the "community" in "community service."

OPPORTUNITIES EVERYWHERE

So first and foremost, the parish needs to catechize that opportunities to serve others and seek justice are all around us every day. The person who is caring for an elderly parent is living out the mission. The stay-at-home mother or father who cooks and cleans and drives four kids every which way is living out the mission. The teenager who puts a stop to bullying, the coworker who speaks out about unethical business behavior, and the parishioner who makes room in the pew for a family of six are all living out the mission. These are all individual opportunities in a greater communal effort to be the Body of Christ.

Of course, there are always needs that only a group of people working together can fill. This is where the parish-coordinated opportunities come in. Local food pantries, soup kitchens, nursing homes, hospitals, homeless shelters, etc., all need volunteers. Life issues, environmental issues, sweatshops, human trafficking, etc., are justice issues that need to be brought to the attention of all parishioners with realistic plans of action. When young people experience these things as a part of a parish community, not only do they learn what is expected of the committed Christian, they learn what is expected of the Christian community as a whole.

Finally, processing the outreach experience before, during, and after the service is very important. The car ride home from a soup kitchen is a perfect opportunity for all to share what they saw, what troubled them, what inspired them, etc. Processing allows us to connect our service to our faith. It helps us recognize that we are more than "social workers," but rather that we are disciples of Jesus called to serve one another as one body. When one part of the body is hurting, the whole body is affected.

Diocesan, State, National, and World Youth Events

This book (as I'm sure you realize by now) is about parish-based youth ministry. It suggests that there is no parish too big or too small, too rich or too poor, too rural or too urban to be able to have its own strong and comprehensive youth ministry. However, many parishes in the United States do depend (sometimes heavily) on the larger Church (their diocese in particular) to provide them with youth ministry programming. One intention of this book is to help parishes like this move away from such a model and move towards its own self-sustaining youth ministry based on an initiation model. This, on the other hand, does not suggest that there is no place for youth participation in the larger Church.

As *a part of* a parish's youth ministry, efforts can be made to participate in diocesan, state, national, and world youth events. These are opportunities for young people to meet the young Church from other parishes, dioceses, and even other countries. It is a direct way of connecting them to the universal Church and a good experiential catechesis of Church structure and solidarity.

Diocesan leadership training, state youth rallies, the National Catholic Youth Conference, and the World Youth Day pilgrimage are all examples of how a parish youth ministry can participate in events of this nature.

Communal Prayer Experiences

Obviously, Mass is the ultimate prayer for the total parish; however, it is also important for a parish to provide additional prayer experiences that extend beyond the celebration of Eucharist. We have already seen how youth experience communal prayer through retreat processes. The question is, what more?

Let's look at the example of Randolph, a sophomore in high school who is active in parish youth ministry. In fact, he does everything that an initiation model calls for concerning the component of prayer and worship. He goes to Mass every week; he goes on the sophomore retreat that incorporates communal, meditative, reflective, and liturgical prayer experiences; he attends every follow-up gathering, which gives him the opportunity to participate in a shared prayer every week; he participates in parish-sponsored service opportunity at least once a month, which always begins and ends with prayer; he goes on a World Youth Day pilgrimage with the opportunity to pray with the young Church led by the pope, and he attends all the family-based mornings of reflection with his parents that also begin and end with prayer. Furthermore, Randolph has been taught to pray

on his own and does so every day. How much more praying is he expected to do?

Assuming that all of Randolph's prayer is authentic, sincere, and ever deepening, there leaves only one major type of prayer that he has yet to experience, prayer with the parish community outside of Mass.

Yes, once again, an Initiation Model of Youth Ministry calls for young people and their families to participate in parish-wide endeavors so as to connect them to the larger faith community. This time we focus on parish prayer services.

As always, the first requirement is collaboration between parish leaders in order to ensure that the prayer service is appropriate for all generations. Take for example a parish lenten reconciliation service (I hate calling it a penance service even though it is technically not wrong to do so). A good parish reconciliation service will be both intergenerational and inspirational. It should be planned with the collaboration of members of all the parish ministries that are affected (youth ministry, music ministry, family ministry, etc.). Of course, if a parish really wants to make the service inspirational, it might have to think out of the box. A simple service of readings and confession may not generate a *metanoia* or heart-changing experience for most people these days, especially young people. This is why a reconciliation service can also include music, ritual action, personal witness, communal prayer, and individual reflection. All of this can be done in many ways and is usually accomplished quite easily as well as enthusiastically by a team of creative staff and parishioners.

Other Command Performances

A colleague of mine brought the phrase "command performance" to our parish from his job at a previous parish. What he means by "command performance" is parish events that not only affect the whole parish community, but events that should be a part of every ministry's calendar. These are events that are publicized by every ministry leader to everyone involved in the respective ministries (which technically in an initiation parish adds up to everyone).

When command performances are put on the youth ministry calendar, youth and their families can truly experience what *Renewing the Vision* refers to as "comprehensive youth ministry." Their experience in parish in not limited to "youth-only" events, and is not only intergenerational, but is interministerial (if that's a word). What I mean is

that "intergenerational" does not always have to be on youth ministry terms. Youth can participate in other parish ministries, just as adults and children can participate in some facets of youth ministry.

We have already established that parish prayer services should be on the calendar as essential aspects of an overall youth ministry. Other command performances could include: parish picnics, parish dinner/dances, parish missions or guest speakers, parish pilgrimages, parish patron saint feast days, etc.

As stated before, by including these things as part of youth ministry, young people and their families are incorporated into the larger faith community, thus counteracting the natural tendency for youth to become "a satellite community connected to the parish in name only."

Social Events, Sports, and Outings

When I was a teenager serving on a parish peer leadership team, we learned about the youth ministry "Wedge Model." Our interpretation of the model (whether interpreted correctly or incorrectly) was that we had to first do "non-churchy" things like ski trips, lock-ins, baseball games, coffee houses, battle of the bands, camping trips, open gyms, CYO basketball teams, bowling, jello wrestling, etc., as a means through which to get young people in the door. From there, we would get some people involved in "semi-churchy" things like service opportunities and parish picnics which in turn would attract even fewer people to be involved in "churchy" things like retreats and going to Mass. Finally, from there, a small group of "ultra-churchy" people (the peer leadership team) would comprise the other end of the wedge and would serve as the catalyst for starting the wedge up again for more people. We understood that everything that happens within the wedge *was* youth ministry.

The goal was to constantly funnel young people through it because the further down the wedge one journeys, more components of youth ministry are experienced; hence, faith continues to be formed.

The wide end of the wedge was always kept wide open with "non-churchy" social events, sports, and outings as a means through which to welcome new people who may not be ready for the more religious types of events and programs and as a stepping stone for the invitation to move further down the wedge.

An Initiation Model of Youth Ministry and the Wedge Model are not far apart in theory. Both incorporate the principles of *Renewing the Vision*, both can consider the life of the parish as the curriculum, and both have no timetables. The main differences, as I see them, are the following.

1. The Wedge Model suggests that the bulk of youth ministry programming should consist of social events, sports, and outings, since these attract the greatest numbers. As we have learned, an Initiation Model is clear to point out that young people and their families must have the opportunity to experience all eight components of youth ministry equally in order for faith to continue to be formed. Social events, sports, and outings are scheduled as a means through which to provide community life and evangelization opportunities.

2. An Initiation Model rejects the notion that "non-churchy" programming is the only way to get young people in the door.

3. The Wedge Model breaks down in areas of the country where young people do not need their parish to provide them with social activities because they get them elsewhere.

Example: Fifteen years ago, my parish used to fill two bus loads of young people for a weekend ski trip each winter. Ten years ago, we were down to two minivan loads. After that, there was no interest, so the annual ski trip became extinct. The reason for this decline was that the young people no longer needed the parish to take them skiing.

This need was being filled by the schools, clubs, and their parents. An initiation model adapts when such trends occur.

Social events, sports, and outings are good youth ministry tools; however, every parish is different. Some parishes use them primarily as evangelization opportunities, while others use them as community-life opportunities. Whether used to get young people in the door or used to provide fun opportunities for those who have already entered through the door, "non-churchy" events and programs do have a place in an Initiation Model of Youth Ministry, but maybe not to the degree of other youth ministry models.

 # Parish Matters

Perhaps by now you have noticed a theme permeating this book: parish matters. The key to effectively and affectively reaching the three goals of Youth Ministry is to ensure that young people and their families experience all eight components in age-appropriate and intergenerational ways and as a part of a parish-wide effort.

Why so much focus on parish? Because as quoted earlier, "The parish is where the Church lives." The parish is the part of the Christian family that we actually know. Parish folk are not those second cousins who live out in the boonies and who we only see at funerals and weddings. These are the people we know and who know us. They are our home, our ongoing Christian community. If youth ministry is not connected with them, it is not really a youth *ministry*, but just a youth *program* that is destined to eventually come to an end.

SECTION FIVE

MARKING THE STAGES

When I was a child, my father used to take me on a train ride every Sunday afternoon (except during football season, of course!) to the end of the line (in our case, either Hoboken or Dover). When we got to the final train station, we would get out, have a hot dog or a hamburger, and then turn around and take the train back home. It was a simple ritual, but it spoke to a reality that would not have been done justice by words alone. My dad could have simply said, "I love you" every Sunday afternoon and left it at that, but the train ritual expressed it with much more depth. The ritual made the reality of my father's love for me more real.

Likewise, religious rituals and symbols make the realities of our faith more present and real to the individual and to the community. They "tap into the sacred" and transcend the ordinary in ways that words cannot. We need not look any further than the baptismal ritual as a good example of this: the plunging into the waters of death and rising to new life; the light of Christ passed on into our hearts; the baptismal garment clothing us in Christ; the chrism oil declaring that we too are anointed ones of God.

Bringing to ritual the various stages of one's faith journey is an essential part of youth ministry. It is not only a connection to the rich tradition of our Church, but a making of time and space in order to recognize, acknowledge, and celebrate the adolescent's faith discovery. Simply saying with words that our faith is continuing to be formed does not express that reality with the same depth as a ritual action.

It should be noted that Sunday Eucharist has been and will continue to be (among other realities) *the* weekly ritual that invites all the baptized to continually recognize, acknowledge, and celebrate our faith development as individuals and as a community. Following is a basic chart to help explain the flow of these rituals.

STAGE	PREPARING TO BE CONFIRMED YOUTH	CONFIRMED YOUTH
1. Come and See	*Rite of Welcoming*	*Welcome to Senior High Youth Ministry Ritual Blessing*
2. Give It a Try	*Rite of Entrance*	*Entrance Ritual Blessing*
3. Keep Going	*Rite of Prayer*	*Lord's Prayer Ritual Blessing*
4. Get Serious	*Rite of Creed*	*Nicene Creed Ritual Blessing*
5. Do You Believe?	*Rite of Covenant*	*Witness Ritual Blessing*
6. I Believe	*Rite of Confirmation* **the Intentional Faith Ritual Blessing can be added to this stage*	*Intentional Faith Ritual Blessing*
7. Time and Talent	*Sunday Eucharist*	*Sunday Eucharist*

In an Initiation Model of Youth Ministry, young people preparing to be confirmed have six different rites or rituals that mark the stages of their faith development and sacramental preparation: The Rite of Welcoming, The Rite of Entrance, The Rite of Prayer, The Rite of Creed, The Rite of Covenant, and the Rite of Confirmation.

For young people who are already confirmed, we also have six ritual blessings that mark the stages of faith development (although not sacramental preparation) and parallel the aforementioned rites: Welcome to Senior High Youth Ministry, Entrance, Lord's Prayer, Nicene Creed, Witness, and Intentional Faith. The first four ritual blessings are almost identical to the paralleled rite; however, the Witness Ritual Blessing is celebrated instead of the Rite of Covenant and the Intentional Faith Ritual Blessing is celebrated in place of the "faith ownership" aspect of confirmation. Both are very different from their counterparts.

Note: those parishes that celebrate confirmation during freshman year or early sophomore year of senior high, may find it necessary to incorporate the Intentional Faith Ritual Blessing into the junior or senior years of youth ministry. If confirmation is celebrated before one is developmentally able to have a full awareness of faith, the Intentional Faith Ritual Blessing can tap into the sacred reality of an owned faith that was not fully present at confirmation.

As we examined earlier, when confirmation is celebrated during late adolescence, the opportunity is there to connect the sacrament to an owned faith.

By the time these rites and ritual blessings are completed, the young people hopefully have gained a deeper appreciation for the Sunday Eucharist through the life of the parish and are more ready than ever to submerge themselves in the rituals and symbols of our liturgy.

FAMILY SHARING

Most rites/ritual blessings are coupled with a family-based morning or evening of reflection so that all can "know what they're doing and why." As stated earlier, the purpose of these rites and ritual blessings is to bring to ritual the experiences that have been a part of the young people's faith journey, and therefore make the reality of what they are experiencing in the present moment more immediate for the whole parish community. The family-based reflections help the young people and their parents grasp the meaning of the ritual more deeply and prepare them to celebrate the rituals more intentionally.

Of course, all of these rites, ritual blessings, and family-based reflections are completely optional. No one and no family is forced to participate. Consequently, those young people who were confirmed in junior high will most likely opt out of all or most of the ritual blessings (especially if the parish has not been using anything close to an initiation model of Church in the past). It may take several years of small percentages of family participation for the majority to discover the value.

Antithetically, the young people who are preparing to be confirmed will most likely initially participate in high percentages due to their parents' still lingering obligatory attitude toward sacraments (I know...this sounds very pessimistic, but my experience and the experience of many other colleagues would suggest that this is the reality of the American Church). In either case, the quality and profundity of the rites and ritual blessings can eventually transform hearts and attitudes so that percentages of participation will not only be high in both cases, but authentic.

 # Welcome to Senior High Youth Ministry

This ritual echoes the beginning of the Rite of Baptism where those who are to be baptized are presented to the Church community by parents and godparents. In this case, since the young people are already baptized, they present themselves at the doors of the church at the beginning of a parish Mass and are welcomed by the community. After Mass, the youth and their parents participate in the welcoming reflection, which serves as an introduction to senior high youth ministry (and, consequently, confirmation preparation for those who have yet to be confirmed).

THE RITE OF WELCOMING
(preparing to be confirmed youth)

Potential candidates gather at the doors of the church with the presider and ministers. If your parish has too many potential candidates for this to be feasible, schedule the Rite of Welcoming at more than one Mass.

Youth Minister My brothers and sisters in Christ, assembled with us this morning are young people from our parish community who are potential candidates for the sacrament of confirmation. Because we are an initiating parish, it is right that we formally and lovingly invite these young members of our community to continue their faith journey to confirmation and beyond, and in doing so, we pledge to continue being witnesses to the gospel and to actively encourage and support them. After Mass this morning, they and their parents have been invited to spend some time here in order to build community and to learn about senior high youth ministry and, consequently, confirmation preparation. Together, let us welcome them. Please direct your attention to the front doors of the church.

Presider Young Christians, what are your names?

Potential candidates pass the microphone, saying their first and last name.

Presider My dear young people, you have joined us today to celebrate Eucharist by right of your baptism; however, you are not fully initiated members of God's Church yet. Your parents, godparents, and this community have taken on the responsibility to bring you up, keeping God's commandments as Christ taught us, by loving God and neighbor. On behalf of our faith community, the parish of ____, I now invite you to consider taking the next step on your journey of faith. "Come and see." We welcome you! (*applause*)

Cantor Please stand and join us in our entrance hymn: _____

Potential candidates join their families in the pews.

Entrance Procession

WELCOME TO SENIOR HIGH YOUTH MINISTRY RITUAL BLESSING (*for confirmed youth*)

Young people gather at the doors of the church with the presider and ministers. If your parish has too many freshmen for this to be feasible, schedule this ritual blessing at more than one Mass

Youth Minister My brothers and sisters in Christ, assembled with us this morning are young people from our parish community who are entering senior high youth ministry. Because we are an initiating parish, it is right that we formally and lovingly invite these young members of our community to continue their faith journey into their high school years and beyond, and in doing so, we pledge to continue being witnesses to the gospel and to actively encourage and support them. After Mass this morning, they and their parents have been invited to spend some time here in order to build community and to learn about senior high youth ministry. Together, let us welcome them. Please direct your attention to the front doors of the church.

Presider Young Christians, what are your names?

Freshmen pass the microphone, saying their first and last name.

Presider My dear young people, you have joined us today to celebrate Eucharist by right of your baptism. Your parents, godparents, confirmation sponsors, and this community have taken on the responsibility to bring you up, keeping God's commandments as Christ taught us, by loving God and neighbor. On behalf of our faith community, the parish of ____, I now invite you to consider taking the next step on your journey of faith. "Come and see." We welcome you! (*applause*)

Cantor Please stand and join us in our entrance hymn: _____

Freshmen join their families in the pews.

Entrance Procession

WELCOMING REFLECTION
(for both preparing to be confirmed and confirmed youth)

» Welcome, Name Tags, Lunch (30 minutes)

After Mass, the young people and their parents are invited to a parish hall. Freshman retreat team leaders can welcome their younger peers and their parents by directing them to the welcome table with available name tags and handouts (although sometimes it is helpful to team leaders if you give them some names tags and a marker and tell them to mingle with both the freshmen and the parents and make them a name tag on the spot). A prepared lunch (perhaps by other members of the parish) awaits those who come in. This is a good opportunity for the freshman retreat team and adult catechists to mingle with the freshmen and their parents.

» Opening Prayer/Introduction (5 minutes)

The opening prayer can take any form. It need not be long but should at least focus on the reason for the gathering. John 1:35–39a ("come and see") is a good focusing scripture for the prayer since the invitation to participate in youth ministry is an invitation to "come and see" where Jesus is staying. Another option would be to use the gospel of the day and connect it to the invitation to get involved. The introduction is simply the speaker introducing himself or herself along with the retreat team and catechists, explaining the schedule of the day and initiating movement.

» Movement (2 minutes)

The youth move into another large area to do large group icebreakers with the retreat team and adult catechists. Parents remain with the coordinator(s) of youth ministry (It's always nice to have the pastor and as many pastoral staff as can make it, but not crucial).

» Large Group Icebreakers (40 minutes)

The team is prepared beforehand to run these "get to know you" icebreakers. The icebreakers chosen should at the very least help all involved get to know each other's names. This is not a time for playing games unless they help the participants get to know one another. Here are two suggestions:

Fruit Basket Upset Everyone sits in a big circle and is assigned a fruit: apple, orange, peach, pear. There is one less seat than people. The person not sitting must introduce him/herself while standing in the middle. Everyone responds, "Hi (insert person's name)!" The person then yells out a fruit. Everyone who has been assigned that fruit must get up and run to the *opposite side* of the circle to find a chair. The person left standing repeats the process. One may also call out "Fruit Basket Upset!" which means that everyone has to get up and run to the other side.

Parallel Lines Two parallel lines of chairs are placed facing each other. Each chair is directly across from another chair (handshake distance away). All chairs are occupied. A leader on a microphone instructs that everyone introduce themselves to the person across from them, shaking that person's hand. The leader then asks a question that provokes more than a one-word answer, and the participants must discuss their answer with the person sitting across from them. After about a minute, the leader instructs one line to stand up and move one seat to the right. The person on the right end stands up and walks to the other end taking the vacant seat all the way on the left. The process is then repeated with a different question. (The questions should be approved by the coordinator of youth ministry before the event.)

» Parent Reflection (40 minutes)

Once the teens are out of the room, ask the parents to sit in groups of about eight. When they are settled, give them this instruction in your own words.

I would like you to discuss with your group why you are here. In other words, what do you hope youth ministry will do for you and your teens? What do you hope to gain from this meeting? What do you want to know? Or if you want me to be most direct: why did you show up here today? I have three requests before you begin discussing. First, please be honest. Second, please do not judge anyone's reason for being here because no matter what anyone says, there's hardly ever a bad reason for coming. Third, I ask that someone in the group be the recorder because I'm going to ask each group to report to the large group.

After no more than ten minutes, ask the groups to give their feedback on what some common responses were in their group. Write their answers on newsprint or an overhead. This should provide a good springboard from which to begin your explanation of senior high youth ministry and consequently confirmation preparation if applicable. A good familiarity with *Renewing the Vision* and of this book in addition to your own wisdom should prove to be enough to deal with all the concerns and hopes of the parents regarding the process.

Although whatever is written on the newsprint will direct the large group conversation, certain elements must be conveyed in case the newsprint does not call for them. These crucial elements are:

- *What is youth ministry?* First of all, it is not a program! It just is! *Youth ministry is ongoing faith formation through which young people and their families live out their baptismal call within the life of the parish* (probably a good idea to put this statement up on the overhead or newsprint). "Ongoing faith formation" means much more than religious instruction. A person's faith is formed primarily through experience. So in order to form your teen in the Christian faith, we not only teach the gospel, but we provide opportunities for you and your teen to experience the gospel, here, at home, and in all areas of life.

- *How do we form faith?* Youth ministry provides opportunities for you and your teens to experience the gospel through eight different components (show Appendix I on overhead). These components, as defined by the U.S. bishops, guide this youth ministry. In other words, every youth ministry event or experience comes under one or more of these components. Actually, most youth ministry opportunities come under more than one heading; for example, the freshman retreat is "community life" because it builds community. It's "catechesis" because the Word of God is echoed throughout the retreat. It's "evangelization" because it can change one's heart. It's "prayer and worship" because we always make time and space to pray and worship. It's "leadership development," especially for the upperclassers on team, and it's "pastoral care" because it fosters compassionate listening and the building of relationships. In order for your teen's faith to continue to be formed, he or she must experience all eight of these components continually during the next four years.

- *Living out our baptismal call* We are all called through our baptism to continue the mission of Jesus. That is our purpose as Catholic Christians—to continue what Jesus started—to share peace and love and light and all those good things with the world. Youth ministry in this parish is a venue through which you and your teens can do that.

- *Youth ministry is a journey* (This section is written using terminology for those parishes that confirm during the senior high years. For parishes with already confirmed senior high youth, simply change your terminology.) Have you ever been on one of those newer airplanes where every seat has its own television screen? I love those because I like to watch the channel that shows a little map of the route my plane is taking. It tells you how high you are and how fast you're going, and there's a little line across the map that shows where you've been. Well, we have one of those just for youth ministry (show youth ministry journey graphic from page 35). Right now, your teens are here (Period of Welcoming). If they decide to move on from here, they will move into the

- *Period of Preparation.* "Preparation for what?" you ask. During this time, they are preparing to one day take ownership of their faith. They do this is by participating in this parish in such a way that they experience all eight components of youth ministry.

AN INTERNSHIP

Consider the Period of Preparation as an internship. They are "learning the ropes," if you will. They are experiencing what it is like to be a Christian so they can base their decision to embrace Christianity on sufficient experience. Once they have had sufficient experience, they move into the Period of Discernment. Here they are asked to look back on their experience in the parish and decide whether or not they wish to continue to do all the things they have been doing, but now by their own choice. And just like some planes are slower than others, some of your teens may need to travel through the preparation period slower than others, and that's fine. Everyone can take it at their own pace. But here's the catch: We do not own any planes that are fast enough to just fly through the preparation period in a month. In fact, according to our diocese, one must prepare for at least __ year(s). So once your teens have discerned themselves to be ready to take ownership of their faith, with our help and guidance, of course, they move into the Period of Celebration. And just like in chapter fifteen of the gospel according to Luke, whenever a coin is lost and then found, or a sheep is lost and then found, or a son is lost and then found, we must celebrate. We call it the Period of Celebration, or in a word: confirmation.

But the journey is not over! Oh no. In fact, in many ways, it's just beginning. After we celebrate, they enter into the Period of Mystagogia, which is an ancient term in the tradition of our Church that means, "grasping the mystery of God." We use it because not only does it sound cool, it accurately describes what is happening at this stage of the journey.

- *Youth Ministry Goals* By the time your teen graduates high school, we want to have accomplished three things (put on overhead or newsprint):
  1. To empower young people to live as disciples of Jesus Christ in our world today.
  2. To draw young people to responsible participation in the life, mission, and work of our parish faith community.
  3. To foster the total personal and spiritual growth of each young person within our parish.

- *Confirmation* (This section is for those parishes that confirm during the senior high years.) You will notice that while I talked about the journey of faith, I only said the word, "confirmation" once. I did that purposely because in this parish the journey that I described would be the same for your teens whether confirmation is celebrated at a senior high level or not. If we didn't celebrate the sacrament at a high school level, we'd probably have to change some of the wording, but the journey would still be the same. What I'm trying to say is that this parish stresses four years of senior high youth ministry. Confirmation preparation *is* participation in youth ministry and post-confirmation *is* participation in youth ministry. There is no "confirmation program" that is separate from youth ministry, no confirmation classes and make-up classes, and no minimum amount of service hours that must be completed and signed for proof in order to be confirmed. There are, however three general requirements (put on overhead or newsprint):

1. One must be open to participation in the parish in such a way that one experiences all eight components of youth ministry.

2. One must experience what it means to be Christian as lived out through our Catholic tradition. In other words, in order to gain knowledge of what a confirmed person is, one must have the opportunity to hear and experience some of the faith stories of the *whole parish community*.

3. One must eventually choose confirmation for oneself just as all other sacraments are choices.

- *Parent Responsibilities* "This is not your father's Oldsmobile." Remember that commercial? Well, what has been described this afternoon is admittedly probably not the approach the Church took when you were young, but it is the way the early Church thought, and experience has shown us that we ought to go back to their mentality. It's a mentality that not only says that parents are the primary faith givers, but provides a structure that allows parents to be this.

Do you remember your child's baptism? You were asked at that baptism if you were willing to form the faith of your child through the Catholic Christian faith tradition. You took on that responsibility and asked the help of your child's godparents. Your presence here today says that you acknowledge and understand that your parish community is also responsible for continuing to form the faith of your teen and is essential to the faith formation of your teen.

And so your parish leadership will provide age-appropriate opportunities for you and this community to continue to form your teen's faith. We on the pastoral staff work for you and with you! We are your servants! We help provide the opportunities, you decide the ones in which to participate in order to live up to the promise that you made at your child's baptism. We provide, you decide! And believe me, there are going to be a lot of opportunities. First and foremost, there is Sunday Mass. Mass is essential. Everything we do flows out of Mass. It is the primary place where faith is formed, and when we as a community celebrate Mass fully, consciously, and actively, there is no better way to pass on our faith tradition. Then, in addition to weekly Mass, we are going to have retreats with weekly follow-up gatherings.

There will also be ample service opportunities that you and your teens can sign up for. We've got diocesan events, prayer services, mornings of reflection, interfaith events, coffee houses, and retreat leader opportunities. There's lector training, minister of communion training, greeter training, youth ministry choir/band, and other parish-wide events. All of this is at your disposal. They cover all eight components of youth ministry. It's all provided to help you pass on the faith. So parent participation is not really asked for or needed or even encouraged. It simply is assumed!

» Teens Rejoin Parents for Concluding Remarks (15 minutes)

Once the teens have rejoined the parents, put up the "four year examples" overhead (Appendix J). The overhead outlines how four years of youth ministry can look for four different kids. Describe each in detail. *(The following examples describe a senior high youth ministry that celebrates confirmation in the middle of the four years. Adaptations can be made for each parish situation.)*

Musical Mike

Musical Mike is the guy who is always in the school musical. From December through March, Musical Mike's time is consumed by school and play practice. He is generally unavailable to get involved in youth ministry during this time period each year. How can parish youth ministry work for him? First of all, he can celebrate Mass every Sunday because there's always time for that. But in terms of his involvement, he participates mostly in the fall (i.e. fall retreats and follow-ups during his ninth and tenth grade years.) All of the liturgical rites and mornings of reflection are held on Sundays so that he and his parents can attend. The service opportunities in which he participates are mostly in the fall and spring, and he sings in the youth ministry choir. His first two years of high school youth ministry are fun, and he enjoys it. He decides that he is ready to take ownership of his faith, so he is confirmed and continues to be involved during his eleventh and twelfth grade years.

Dancing Debra

Dancing Debra has dance lessons every Tuesday and Thursday night and recitals quite often on Saturdays, especially in the fall and spring. In addition to celebrating Eucharist every week with her family, she decides to participate in the winter retreat processes during her ninth and tenth grade years because she has the most free time during the winter and because the winter retreats offer follow-ups on Sunday and Monday nights, which fit into her schedule. She and her parents make the liturgical rites and the mornings of reflection a priority, and together they participate in service opportunities and parish events. Debra is even able to set aside a long weekend to participate in the National Catholic Youth Conference with other teens and adults from the parish. She has a great experience in youth ministry and chooses to confirm her faith through the sacrament of confirmation. She discerns a call to become a minister of communion and a call to work with children through the family ministry. Her experience at NCYC prompts her to go to World Youth Day.

Soccer Sam

Soccer Sam is an all-state soccer player. He plays year round. His parents support him in his desire to be the best soccer player, but they are not regular churchgoers. Sam likewise does not celebrate Mass with great frequency. He and his parents participate in the mornings of reflection and the rites during his ninth grade and he went on the freshman retreat but didn't go to any follow-ups. Soccer was just more important than anything else. It looked like he wasn't going to reach a point where confirmation would make sense. Then he went on the mission week during the summer between his ninth and tenth grade years and had a conversion.

He realized that he wanted to have a deeper faith, so he paid more attention during the mornings of reflection, put more of himself into the spring sophomore retreat and follow-ups, became a dependable volunteer at all of the mission fundraisers and even started to get his parents to go to Mass more often with him. He did indeed celebrate confirmation and became a lector and continued to make time for the mission week and fundraisers. And he didn't miss a beat with his soccer commitments. He made it work.

Marching Band Martha

Marching Band Martha never registered for youth ministry during her freshman year. Her parents did not believe in forcing a religion upon their children, so naturally, Martha chose not to participate in her parish during her ninth grade. Interestingly enough, all of her friends were involved in youth ministry and got a lot out of it. By tenth grade, Martha decided that if her friends thought it was cool, then she would give it a try. She got involved, mostly in what her friends were doing, but confirmation wasn't even on her mind. By the end of tenth grade, she realized that her friends were right and now she wants to be confirmed. So she does all the rites during her junior year plus a whole bunch of other things and sure enough, she confirms her baptism at the end of her junior year. She continues to stay involved and becomes a very important youth ministry leader.

The point of these four examples is that youth ministry can look different for everyone. There is no "one size fits all." Our job is to provide you with ample opportunities throughout each of your four years so that you can create your own youth ministry schedule that utilizes your gifts and talents and helps you grow in your faith.

LIKE RIDING A BIKE

So here is my advice on how to get started in youth ministry. I want all the young people here to recall when they first learned how to ride a bike. Parents, try to recall that day as well. (It helps to have team leaders act this out with a real bike as you are describing it.) Parents, remember at first you had to hold your sons and daughters upright until they found their balance. They wobbled those first few feet while trying to work up the confidence. Some probably caught on quickly, others needed more pushing, but eventually they all began to ride without any help. Well, the same goes for youth ministry.

Parents, you just may have to push your teen to get involved at first. Some will need more pushing and holding up than others, but eventually, you have to let go. And you will know the right time to let go. We are so confident in the way that we do youth ministry that we know that everyone who participates with an open mind will eventually want to participate without prodding from parents. But for starters, parents, by all means, prod away!

» **Witness by upperclassers (10 minutes)**
Topic: My youth ministry involvement and what I got out of it.

It's important for the potential candidates to hear from their peers who have participated in youth ministry in the way we are asking them to participate.

» **Questions (10 minutes)**
These should be fielded by the youth minister, the catechists, and the team, depending on who can best answer.

» **Announcements/Sign-ups (10 minutes)**
- Schedules, retreat applications, youth ministry registration available
- Service sign-ups: Every week in vestibule of the Church
- Initial interview: Schedule meeting with a catechist or staff member (Appendix C)

» **Closing Prayer (2 minutes)**
There is no need for a long, reflective prayer at this point. The people have been sitting for two hours. A short prepared prayer or spontaneous prayer will suffice.

Entrance

This ritual was first introduced by Thomas Zanzig in his confirmation preparation work entitled: *Confirmed in a Faithful Community* (Coordinator's Manual, p. 111). In the process that Zanzig lays out, the Rite of Entrance ritual marks the beginning of what he refers to as the "Period of Formation." It is an adaptation of the RCIA Rite of Acceptance and serves as an opportunity for the young people to formally acknowledge that they are willing to continue to be formed in the way of Christ by their faith community. It is also a chance for the faith community to acknowledge the first-year candidates and express support and prayer. The model of youth ministry as spelled out in *this* book likewise utilizes the Rite of Entrance/Entrance Ritual Blessing as a rite of passage from one period to another (namely the Period of Welcoming to the Period of Preparation or the Come and See Stage to the Give it a Try Stage) where young people express their willingness to continue to be formed and the parish offers support and prayer. However, the ritual to be described in this book does not have much in common with either the Rite of Acceptance or Zanzig's version of the Rite of Entrance. The purpose is the same, but the ritual

is very different. Moreover, it is the suggestion of this book that the Rite of Entrance/Entrance Ritual Blessing be celebrated at the closing liturgy at the freshman retreat (which should be scheduled at a regular weekend parish Mass). As described earlier, the freshman retreat (which is best held on church grounds) serves as the "igniter," an experience that helps freshmen feel more at ease or even on fire with the idea of participating in youth ministry on an ongoing basis. The young people have just had a faith experience that has brought them to a point in their faith journeys where they can sincerely express their willingness to continue to be formed in the way of Christ by their parents and parish community. When a freshman retreat does what it is supposed to do, there is no better time to celebrate the Rite of Entrance/Entrance Ritual Blessing.

Note: If your parish offers more than one option for a freshman retreat, the Rite of Entrance/ Entrance Ritual Blessing can be celebrated at the end of each retreat. When young people come forward for participation in youth ministry any time after ninth grade, an additional Rite of Entrance/Entrance Ritual

Blessing can be scheduled at a parish liturgy during an appropriate time of year (perhaps after the person(s) in question have experienced their own age-appropriate retreat).

THE RITE OF ENTRANCE

The first-year candidates are pre-seated.

The following should be included in the Rite of Entrance booklets that are distributed in the pews:

The sacraments of initiation (baptism, confirmation, and Eucharist) celebrate our memberships within the Church. At baptism, the parents and godparents of our candidates promised, by their example, to raise these young people to be living witnesses of the faith through our Catholic tradition.

Today we celebrate the Rite of Entrance, which marks the beginning of the journey for our youth who are moving toward the completion of the sacraments of initiation. Our first-year candidates express their willingness to become more actively involved in their faith life.

They cannot do it alone. We, the community of ___, journey with them to their celebration of confirmation.

May they always experience the love and support of our parish family.

RITE OF ENTRANCE RITUAL

Presider My brothers and sisters, our young people gathered with us today have come forward to express their desire to begin preparation for the sacrament of confirmation. By continuing to be active members of this parish community nourished by the Eucharist, they hope to one day stand before us and *confirm* their baptismal promise to be the light of the world. And so I ask all of you who are assembled in community today to

speak on behalf of our entire parish family: Will you welcome and actively support these young people and continue to be faith witnesses to them as they journey toward confirmation and beyond?

All We will.

Presider I now ask the parents of our candidates to please stand.

Parents, you stand today as you did on the day of your child's baptism. Your presence with them is a symbol that you have taken seriously their baptismal promise. Your continuing witness and support will be needed more than ever in the years to come. However, the time is approaching when these young people will accept and embrace for themselves all that you have handed on to them.

And so I ask you, their parents: Will you continue to be witnesses to the gospel for your sons and daughters, and will you encourage them to deepen the faith which you have passed on to them?

Parents We will.

Presider I now invite our sponsor catechists and freshman retreat team leaders to come forward and receive the light from our baptismal candle. (*Light candles.*)

Our young people and adults have made the commitment to pass on the light of their faith to our candidates this year. They too will witness to our faith and journey with them.

And now I ask all first-year candidates to please come forward.

Candidates come forward, take candle, stand on either side of catechists facing the people.

This whole community has expressed its support and encouragement for you as you begin this journey.

And so I ask you: Are you open to be formed in the way of the gospel through actively participating in this parish?

First Year Candidates We are.

Presider Receive the light of Christ as a sign of your willingness.

Light is passed on.

Youth Minister Speaking on behalf of all candidates, what do you hope to gain during the next two years of preparation?

Two to four predetermined candidates answer the question on microphone.)

Presider Loving Father, your Son taught us to be the light of the world. May these young people gathered with us today truly be children of the light. May their preparation for confirmation and beyond show them how to make their hearts shine with the love of Christ. Amen.

ENTRANCE RITUAL BLESSING

The freshmen are pre-seated.

The following should be included in the worship aid booklets that are distributed in the pews:

An initiating parish continuously recognizes its responsibility to be living witnesses of the faith for one another through the Catholic tradition, especially for its young members. Even after our confirmation, the conversion process continues and must be nourished by a faithful community.

Today we will celebrate an Entrance Ritual Blessing, which signifies two things:

1. The willingness of our freshmen to continue to be formed in faith by this parish community through participation in senior high youth ministry.

2. The willingness of this parish community to continue being clear and active witnesses to our freshmen as their faith deepens and grows.

May they always experience the love and support of our parish community.

RITUAL BLESSING

Presider My brothers and sisters, our young people gathered with us today have come forward to express their desire to begin their involvement in senior high youth ministry. By continuing to be active members of this parish community nourished by the Eucharist, they hope to one day stand among us with faith that is fully owned and intentional.

And so I ask all of you who are assembled in community today to speak on behalf of our entire parish family: Will you welcome and actively support these young people and continue to be faith witnesses to them as they journey toward owned faith and beyond?

All We will.

Presider I now ask the parents of our candidates to please stand.

Parents, you stand today as you did on the day of your child's baptism. Your presence with them is a symbol that you have taken seriously their baptismal promise. Your continuing witness and support will be needed more than ever in the years to come.

However, the time is approaching when these young people will accept and embrace for themselves all that you have handed on to them.

And so I ask you, their parents: Will you continue to be witnesses to the gospel for your sons and daughters, and will you encourage them to deepen the faith which you have passed on to them?

Parents We will.

Presider I now invite our catechists and freshman retreat team leaders to come forward and receive the light from our baptismal candle. (*Light candles.*)

Our young people and adults have made the commitment to pass on the light of their faith to our freshmen this year. They too will witness to our faith and journey with them.

And now I ask all freshman retreat candidates to please come forward.

Candidates come forward, take candle, stand on either side of catechists facing the people.

This whole community has expressed its support and encouragement for you as you begin this journey.

And so I ask you: Are you open to be formed in the way of the gospel through actively participating in this parish and this parish's youth ministry?

First Year Candidates We are.

Presider Receive the light of Christ as a sign of your willingness.

Light is passed on.

Youth Minister Speaking on behalf of all our candidates, what do you hope to gain during the next four years of senior high youth ministry?

Two to four predetermined candidates answer the question.

Presider Loving Father, your Son taught us to be the light of the world. May these young people gathered with us today truly be children of the light. May their participation in senior high youth ministry show them how to make their hearts shine with the love of Christ. Amen.

Lord's Prayer

As the young people are engaging themselves in the life of the parish through youth ministry, it is important to acknowledge that they are moving along in their faith journey toward the next stage. The parish has already welcomed the young people and has invited them to give youth ministry a try, and they have done so. It is now time to encourage them to keep going; therefore, the next stage in an Initiation Model of Youth Ministry is appropriately named, "The Keep Going Stage." The Rite of Prayer/Lord's Prayer Ritual Blessing is the ritual that marks this rite of passage. Once again, we parallel the RCIA process which ritualizes the presentation of the Lord's Prayer to the elect.

However, there are considerable differences between this ritual and the RCIA ritual. The young candidates have been praying the Lord's Prayer their whole lives. It need not be presented to them. What is needed, on the other hand, is an acknowledgment of this prayer's presence and effect on their lives, as well as a challenge for them to deepen their understanding of the words they pray. Most of us learn the Lord's Prayer as children, but in many ways, it is an adult prayer. The morning of reflection that precedes the Mass at which this ritual takes place deals with this

very issue. The young people with their parents are called to reflect on the words of the prayer and try to deepen their understanding of it. Then later, at Mass, the community acknowledges and celebrates their effort by praying with them in a deliberate way the prayer that Jesus taught us. As the catechism teaches, the Lord's Prayer is the "summary of the whole gospel" (#2761). The Rite of Prayer/Lord's Prayer Ritual Blessing is therefore also a means through which the young people express their willingness to be an essential part of the prayer life of the parish community. It is highly recommended that the Rite of Prayer/Lord's Prayer Ritual Blessing be scheduled some time during the lenten season, since prayer is one of the main focuses of Lent. Also, for those preparing for confirmation, Lent is a natural time for the parish to remember and acknowledge its young people preparing for full initiation.

RITE OF PRAYER/LORD'S PRAYER MORNING OF REFLECTION

9:30 AM Welcome (preferably by the retreat teams that have been ministering to this age group during the year.)

Juice, coffee, water

Name tags
Muffins, bagels optional

9:40 AM Focusing Activity

- Divide everyone up into circles of about eight or nine people (three to four families per group), but keep everyone in the same room.

- Ask them to go around the circle and each introduce themselves.

- Ask everyone to watch the following scene from *Bruce Almighty* closely.

- Show the scene from *Bruce Almighty* toward the end, where Bruce stands before God and prays that his girlfriend have a happy life.

- Ask all to once again go around the circle and each share with the group the last unselfish prayer that they made.

- When all have had a chance to share, ask the large group if anyone said that the last unselfish prayer that they made was the Lord's Prayer.

- If anyone raises a hand, ask that person why and use the answer to transition into your introduction of the Lord's Prayer. If no one raises a hand, simply take that opportunity to state that most of us probably could have raised our hands because the Lord's Prayer is the ultimate unselfish prayer and the most common Christian prayer.

9:55 AM Introduction

Purpose of the morning: To reflect on the Our Father and how it is a model of prayer for adult Christians and no longer a childhood prayer.

"You may look through all the prayers in the scriptures, but you will not find anything that is not contained in the Lord's Prayer." (St. Augustine)

Introduce and proclaim the two versions: Luke 11:1–4 and Matthew 6:9–13.

10:00 AM Begin reflection on the Our Father.

Give each person the handout (while they remain in their groups). Explain the significance of the first section of the prayer (see leaders' catechesis guide) followed by an invitation for each person to rewrite in his or her own words that section. After that, have them share with their group what they wrote. Repeat this process for each section of the prayer (Explanation—Rewrite—Discussion). When finished, instruct the groups to go back and create one prayer based on the consensus of the group. Show them a couple of examples for help (perhaps from last year or from your own research).

10:35 AM Conclusion (to be put into your own words) Now that we have reflected on the Lord's Prayer, hopefully we have all come to a deeper appreciation of its depth. The challenge for us is to think more intently about the words we pray. Perhaps even slow down a little. A young novice once asked Teresa of Avila, "Mother, what shall I do to become a contemplative?" Teresa immediately responded, "Say the Our Father—but take an hour to say it." That pretty much sums up the purpose of today's reflection. In a few minutes, we are going to celebrate Mass together with our parish community. When we get to the part of Mass when we pray the Lord's Prayer, we will begin the Rite of Prayer/Lord's Prayer Ritual. Keep in mind that when we pray the Lord's Prayer together, all will be asked to pray it much more slowly than we usually pray it, so as to be consistent with today's message.

10:40 AM Rehearsal of Ritual

10:45 AM Closing Prayer

- Dim lights, candle

- Proclaim Luke 11:1–4

- Each group has a representative read its prayer

- Proclaim Matthew 6:9–13

- May this reflection lead us all to a deeper and more meaningful prayer life. Amen.

11:00 AM Mass

INSTRUCTION: After hearing and reflecting on the explanation of each section of the Lord's Prayer, rewrite that section in your own words so that it makes sense to you. *Do not jump ahead!*

Our Father who art in heaven

Hallowed be thy name

Thy kingdom come

Thy will be done on earth as it is in heaven

Give us this day our daily bread

And forgive us our trespasses as we forgive those who trespass against us

And lead us not into temptation

But deliver us from evil.

LEADER'S CATECHESIS GUIDE FOR THE LORD'S PRAYER

The following reflection on the Lord's Prayer is based on many sources, but no one in particular. In one sense, it is my translation of the Catechism's teaching on the Lord's Prayer, but it is also heavily influenced by lectures that I have heard in person from Michael Himes, Eugene LaVerdiere, Paul Bernier, and Richard Rohr. In other words, I put their thoughts into my own words so that you may put them into your own words.

Our Father Who Art in Heaven

We begin the prayer with the epitome of Christian unselfishness: "Our Father." First and foremost, the God of Jesus is not about "God and me." The God of Jesus is about "God and we." The God that we profess our faith in is "our" God. Jesus teaches that God is not only *my* personal God, but the God of all. God is in all, of all, and for all without conditions. None of us have special privileges with God as if God listens to one person more than another. Understanding God as "our" God, suggests that our faith is much more than personal. It suggests that we must have a communal relationship with God (that is, look for the presence of God in our lives through community).

And so Jesus teaches us to call God, "Father who art in heaven." The Hebrew word that Jesus used was "Abba," which translates better into English as "Daddy." It is a term of endearment that one uses for one's father, but there is a distinction between how a child uses the word and how adults use the word. Imagine that there is an old man with a grown-up son and a grown-up daughter. The son goes across the country to bring his father back to move in with him and his family. He asks his sister to look after the kids while he is gone. After a week of moving, the son with his father finally makes it back home. When they pull into the driveway, the kids run out of the house yelling, "Abba, Abba!" They are followed by their aunt who walks up to her father, smiles and says, "Abba!" as she hugs him. The aunt's "Abba" was different than the kids'

"Abba." It had more history, more intimacy, and more complexity to it. This is the kind of "Abba" we refer to when we call our God "Father." Our God is like a loving parent who has taught us all we know, has brought us up and has loved us unconditionally through the good times and the bad. This is the kind of God that Jesus teaches us to image in heaven. Furthermore, understanding God as a loving parent suggests that we are all brothers and sisters and should treat one another as such.

Hallowed Be Thy Name

It almost seems silly to pray that God's name be holy. Shouldn't that just be a given? Why do we need to ask God to never stop being God? What makes us think that God would even consider not being holy even for a minute? But this is not a selfish prayer. *We ask that God's name remain holy for all so that all may put God before themselves.* If you still think it's silly to pray this, ask yourself how many times in your life you put other things ahead of God. Take celebrating Mass for example. Is celebrating Mass with your parish a priority in your life or do you fit it in when you don't have anything else to do like sports or work? Do you sometimes consider worldly things holier than God? I do. I try not to, but sometimes I do. That is why it is important to pray that God's name be holy, not for God's sake, but for our sake.

Thy Kingdom Come

Here we pray that the kingdom of God be made a reality to us primarily through the second coming of Christ. But don't think of it as praying for the end of the world (which is essentially what we believe comes with the second coming of Christ). Think of it as praying that we may experience the fullness of grace in the next world. We are not so much concerned with *how* God's kingdom comes to us, but *that* it comes to us. But this part of the prayer almost sounds selfish. It almost sounds like we are asking God to give us heaven so that we may be happy. This is where we as disciples of Jesus must remember that the kingdom of God is not something for which we just sit around and wait. The kingdom of God is something that we are called to build here and now. It is right smack in front of us, but not all of it, which leads right into the next petition in the prayer.

Thy Will Be Done on Earth as It Is in Heaven

We pray that God's will (love, peace, justice, and all those good things) be in its fullness here on Earth just as it is in heaven. "Heaven on earth," is the phrase that comes to mind. But, as suggested earlier, this part of the prayer is not just us asking God for something and then sitting back and waiting to see if it happens. We are also not praying that God magically make all sin and difficulty go away because that would mean we lose our free will. How is God's will done on Earth then? It is only done through God's creatures who have the ability to understand God's will. We are those creatures. As far as we know, we are the only creatures who know and understand God's will. So here we pray that all *do* the fullness of God's will so that all may experience the fullness of God (heaven on earth).

Give Us This Day Our Daily Bread

This is probably the most misunderstood part of the Lord's Prayer primarily because it was very difficult to translate from its original form. However, one thing is clear: it has something to do with Eucharist. More specific, it has something to do with the hospitality aspect of Eucharist. Think of two very different groups of friends sitting in a school cafeteria during lunch. One group sits in the corner and is very private. They do not let just anyone sit with them. In fact, they do not talk to or even look at anyone whom they deem unworthy to sit with them. The other group of friends, however, sit right in the middle of the cafeteria. They all are very easy to approach, and they will talk to anyone. Everyone in the school knows that all are welcome to sit with them at their lunch table. Even the private kids who sit in the corner are invited. Every day, those who sit in the corner become more and more secluded and more and more disconnected

from the rest of their classmates. On the other hand, those who sit in the middle become more and more connected to one another. The meal that both groups share becomes symbolic of the type of people that they are becoming. The kids in the corner are becoming closed and disconnected individuals while the kids in the middle are becoming a welcoming and hospitable community. "Give us this day our daily bread" is a petition that we may recognize within ourselves every day the ability to share ourselves with one another the way the kids at the middle lunch table share their lunch.

And Forgive Us Our Trespasses as We Forgive Those Who Trespass Against Us

There it is. We pray this petition all the time, but how many of us actually stop and think about what we are praying? Of course, it wouldn't seem like a real prayer if we didn't ask God to forgive us for the times when we have sinned. We are used to doing this. It's not a big deal to us in this day and age. But here we actually put a condition on our prayer. Do you see it? It's right in front of us! Here we are asking God to forgive us, but only to the degree that we forgive others! Imagine if we put these conditions on all aspects of our lives: may we eat only as much as we feed others; may we be sheltered in homes only to the degree that we shelter others; may we be loved only to the degree that we love others. Truly this part of the Lord's Prayer is as the Catechism claims: "astonishing."

And Lead Us Not into Temptation

Did you ever notice that often in the gospels, Jesus refers to himself as the Son of Man and not the Son of God? Why does he do this? Well, first of all, "Son of Man" literally means, "the human one." Why would Jesus call himself "the human one" when we all know that he is the divine one? The answer is the same reason why he teaches us to pray this petition. Jesus accepts and embraces his humanity because being human is good. In fact, according to the book of Genesis, when God created humans, God saw them to be "very good." However, there always seems to be the temptation to look at ourselves and think of ourselves as not very good or worthy or sacred. Jesus accepted his humanity and everything that comes with it, even death. Jesus teaches us through his life that fully accepting ourselves for who God made us to be is the path to eternal life. It is only those times when we give into the temptation to not be ourselves that cause us to stray from that path. Here we pray that God may lead us in the way of fully accepting ourselves for who we are.

But Deliver Us from Evil

Here we pray that our Father deliver us from the evil one, whom we refer to as "Satan." But Satan is not what popular culture would depict: a red guy with horns and a tail and a pitchfork. Satan, in the Judeo-Christian tradition is the "tempter." Satan is the one who forever says, "no," to everything. If Satan had his way (or her way), nothing except God would exist because according to Satan, if you are not God, you are not worthy of existence. It is better to be nothing than to be anything other than God. Everything that is not God is junk and doesn't even deserve to be, according to Satan. God, on the other hand, is the opposite. According to God, all of existence is good, and humans are not just good but are very good. The evil one can so easily tempt us to look at things and deem them unworthy of existence. The evil one can and has tempted humanity to look at itself and conclude that others are unworthy of existence. We ask that our Father deliver us from allowing Satan to penetrate and shape our attitudes. May we see ourselves and all of creation as God sees it.

Amen: It is so!

THE RITE OF PRAYER

After the Great Amen, the priest says the following:

Presider When the disciples saw Jesus "praying in a certain place," they waited until he was finished and asked him to teach them how to pray. Their image of God had been turned upside down by this man from Galilee, and they were unsure how to express their new and more intimate relationship with the Lord. Jesus responded by teaching them the Lord's Prayer.

This morning, our first-year candidates for confirmation and their parents spent time reflecting on the Lord's Prayer. I now invite them to join me around the altar.

Candidates and parents assemble around the altar behind the priest.

Presider Like the first disciples, we are invited to deepen our understanding of our image of God. Let us join with our candidates in their reflection by taking some added time today, by slowing down and reflectively praying the Lord's Prayer together. I invite all of us gathered here to open our hands as a sign that we are open to the God who *is* the absolute mystery that grounds and supports all that exists. And so as brothers and sisters in Christ, let us pray together in one voice the words that Jesus taught us.

All Our Father...

Presider Deliver us, Lord, from every evil, and grant us peace in our day. In your mercy keep us free from sin and protect us from all anxiety as we wait in joyful hope for the coming of our Savior, Jesus Christ.

All For the kingdom, the power and the glory are yours, now and forever.

Presider Lord Jesus Christ, you said to your apostles: I leave you peace, my peace I give you. Look not on our sins, but on the faith of your Church, and grant us the peace and unity of your kingdom where you live and reign for ever and ever.

All Amen.

Presider The peace of the Lord be with you always.

All And also with you.

Presider or Deacon Let us offer one another the sign of peace.

All offer a sign of peace. Candidates and parents return to their seats.

THE LORD'S PRAYER RITUAL BLESSING

After the Great Amen, the priest says the following:

Presider When the disciples saw Jesus "praying in a certain place," they waited until he was finished and asked him to teach them how to pray. Their image of God had been turned upside down by this man from Galilee, and they were unsure how to express their new and more intimate relationship with the Lord. Jesus responded by teaching them the Lord's Prayer.

This morning, our freshmen and their parents spent time reflecting on the Lord's Prayer. I now invite them to join me around the altar.

Freshmen and Parents assemble around the altar behind the priest.

Presider Like the first disciples, we are invited

to deepen our understanding of our image of God. Let us join with our candidates in their reflection by taking some added time today, by slowing down and reflectively praying the Lord's Prayer together. I invite all of us gathered here to open our hands as a sign that we are open to the God who *is* the absolute mystery that grounds and supports all that exists. And so as brothers and sisters in Christ, let us pray together in one voice the words that Jesus taught us.

All Our Father...

Presider Deliver us, Lord, from every evil, and grant us peace in our day. In your mercy keep us free from sin and protect us from all anxiety as we wait in joyful hope for the coming of our Savior, Jesus Christ.

All For the kingdom, the power and the glory are yours, now and forever.

Presider Lord Jesus Christ, you said to your apostles: I leave you peace, my peace I give you. Look not on our sins, but on the faith of your Church, and grant us the peace and unity of your kingdom where you live and reign for ever and ever.

All Amen.

Presider The peace of the Lord be with you always.

All And also with you.

Presider or Deacon Let us offer each other the sign of peace.

All offer a sign of peace. Candidates and parents return to their seats.

Nicene Creed

This ritual at Sunday liturgy is preceded by a family-based morning of reflection. It is recommended that it be scheduled on the Feast of Christ the King. The young people are now moving from the "keep going" stage to the "get serious" stage. They are now developmentally and spiritually more able to seriously reflect on the tenets of our faith. In other words, they are moving from a "faith given" toward a "faith owned." The morning of reflection strongly challenges the young people to reflect on how the Nicene Creed is truly what they believe and not just memorized words.

The end of the Church Year (Christ the King) is a good time for this reflection. Even though the readings are apocalyptic and difficult to translate into "teenage language," the fact that we are ending the year and contemplating the coming of the kingdom makes the Feast of Christ the King the most appropriate day to celebrate this rite. In many ways, reflecting on the "end time" is a time in the "right now" to "get serious." During the morning of reflection, parents are given the task of reflecting with their sons and daughters on the different sections of the Nicene Creed. At Mass, both parents and candidates are called up into the sanctuary (or in front if space is limited) to profess the Creed with the worshipping community as always. This allows the community to profess with the families as well as acknowledge the young people who are more seriously than ever trying to write the words on their hearts.

RITE OF CREED/NICENE CREED MORNING OF REFLECTION

9:30 AM Welcome (preferably by the retreat teams that have been ministering to this age group during the year.)

 Juice, coffee, water

 Name tags

 Muffins, bagels optional

9:40 AM Icebreaker: I Believe…

9:50 AM Prayer

Leader	The Lord is with us.
All	Now and forever.
Leader	Lord, open our eyes, open our ears, and open our hearts.
All	And we will live your Word.

Scripture

Matthew 25:31–46 (Year A)

John 18:33b–37 (Year B)

Luke 23:35–43 (Year C)

Silent reflection

Leader Let us pray.

All Lord Jesus,
You are the King of Compassion,
The King of Justice,
The King of Hope,
And the King of Love.
May your kingdom come into our lives,
And into our hearts.
May we be open
To the faith that you give us,
And to the faith that we profess each
week.
May we become living creeds
To one another.
For this we pray to you,
Our Lord and Savior,
living and reigning,
With the Father and through the Spirit
Now and forever.
Amen.

9:55 AM Introduction (to be put in your own words) So here we are at the end of the Church year: the Feast of Christ the King. Beginning with Advent last year, all throughout Ordinary Time and Lent and Easter, we have heard the "Jesus Story." We have journeyed with Jesus. We have been with him in his ministry, in his dying and in his rising. We know who Jesus is, and we know that his story is our story. The Church calls this the Paschal Mystery. And now we have come to the end, and we are called to consider when "Jesus will come again in glory to judge the living and the dead, and his kingdom will have no end." In other words, today reminds us to get serious. We are challenged to get serious about our faith and ask ourselves some tough questions. Do we really believe? If so,

do our lives reflect what we believe? This is what we are here to do this morning: to reflect on what we say we believe (more specifically, to reflect on the Nicene Creed that we profess each week) and to challenge ourselves and each other to live in accordance with what we believe.

Recap: You may recall this picture that I showed you last year (picture from page 35 or 42). This is our little journey of faith diagram depicting the different periods of the youth ministry journey. Right now you are smack dab in the middle of the Period of Preparation (wording will be different if you are working with confirmed youth). However, you will recall that the Period of Preparation is divided into three stages: the "give it a try" stage, the "keep going" stage, and the "get serious" stage (show Appendix K). And guess what? It is time to move into the "get serious" stage. You have given youth ministry a try and have stuck with it until this point. Now this parish is asking you to take a much more serious look at your faith. The place to start is with the tenets of our faith which are summed up in the Nicene Creed (distribute *The Profession of Faith* handout). Parents, this is the faith that you have been passing on to your sons and daughters. It was given to all of us at baptism. Now it is time for us to continue to pass on our Creed, but now at a deeper level than ever before. Why?

Option 1: Because this is the belief that you will confirm should you decide to celebrate the sacrament of confirmation. We must make the Creed real and understandable before we can confirm our belief in it.

Option 2: Because this is the belief that you "confirmed" at your confirmation. We must continue to make the Creed real and understandable as we confirm our belief in it.

10:00 AM Divide into four groups (or eight groups, twelve groups, sixteen groups, etc., depending on the size of the group) Each group should consist of four to six family units. Give each group an assignment sheet. Explain that we have divided the Nicene Creed into four sections. Explain that each group is responsible for reflecting on *one* of the four sections. Have each group elect a leader to read aloud to their group their section of the Creed, the assignment directions, and to record their answers. Be available to go around to answer any questions. They have ten minutes.

10:10 AM Report to Large Group: As each group reports their answers, write them on the transparency (you may have to change a word or two into a different form in order for it to make sense; for example, group one chooses the word, "love," to describe God. Under "We Believe in God, the..." you could write "source of love" or "presence of love" or "ground of our love." Get it? As each group reports what words or phrases they have come up with, you may want to seize upon the teaching moments. Here are some examples I have used in the past:

A QUESTION MARK

Group 1 says that God is a big question mark. Believe it or not, this is actually the official Church teaching: God is first and foremost a big question mark. The word that the Church uses, however, is "mystery." God is first and foremost mystery. In other words, God is so vast, so deep, and so beyond our comprehension, that we must admit that most of God has not been revealed to us yet. God is not a mystery to be solved, rather, God is something that we know deeply, yet we are always growing deeper into God. My scripture professor in college, Fr. Eugene LaVerdiere, compared the mystery of God to his parents' relationship with each other. He said that one time he went home to visit his parents, who have been married over fifty years, and was sitting at the kitchen table for breakfast one morning. His father, reading the newspaper looked over to his mother and said, "You know?" Then there was silence. The mother later replied, "Yeah, I know." The two had come to know each other so well, that they didn't even need to use complete sentences to communicate. But then, later on a walk, his father said to him, "You know, Gene, your

mother is always full of surprises." The point: God is someone that we know really well, but is always full of surprises. It's the "always full of surprises" part of God that we the Church refer to as mystery.

A FRIEND

Group 2 says that Jesus is a friend. Jesus is indeed our friend who reveals God to us. Perhaps a story may help: There once was a little boy who used to go visit his grandparents in the country every summer. His grandparents had lots of land and a small pond with ducks in the front yard. Every morning, the little boy would have his breakfast and then run outside to play with the ducks. But the ducks would always swim away when he came near. This made the boy very sad. So one day, he decided to bring some bread to feed the ducks. And sure enough, the ducks didn't swim away, but stayed for the food. After the bread was gone, the boy thought to himself, "Finally I get to play with the ducks!" So he jumped in the pond with them, but again they all swam away even though he had just fed them. The poor little boy tried this every day of every summer until one day he gave up. Then some years later, when he was almost a man, he sat on the front porch of the house one summer day, and he watched the ducks in the pond. He remembered how he used to always want to play with those ducks as a child, but they would never play with him. Then he came to a revelation: those ducks would never accept him, even if he fed them, because he was not one of them. The only way those ducks would play with him would be if he became a duck. Moral of the story: God became one of us in Jesus not only to feed us, but to be our friend. There is no need to run away.

THE SPIRIT IS EXPERIENCE

Group 3 says that the Holy Spirit is experienced through the encouragement of friends and family: In John's version of the gospel, the Holy Spirit is referred to as, "The Paraclete." There is no equivalent in English; however, it can be translated as meaning, "the Spirit of God that spurs us on" (Himes p. 41). In other words, the Paraclete is the one who tells us to keep going, to never give up. I remember one time when I was a senior in high school. I was on the football team and playing in a game on a cold and rainy day. It was the fourth quarter and we were getting killed. I was cold and wet and covered in mud, and of course our offense had turned the ball over once again.

To make matters worse, my job the whole day was to cover a huge all-state tight end who at this point was just taking running starts at trying to level me into the ground on running plays. I distinctly remember wanting to give up at that point, and well I might have if not for something that happened. From my right side I heard cheering. It was coming from my teammates on the bench and from the cheerleaders behind them and from the friends and family in the stands behind them. They would not let us quit, even when all hope for victory was gone. They were standing and cheering as if the game were close, while most of the fans from the other team had retreated from the rain. They spurred me on and gave me the strength to not give up. This is what we mean by "Paraclete." This is how the Spirit of God is present in our world.

LEAD BY EXAMPLE

Group 4 says that the Church should lead by example. I remember one time when I was in my early 20s, a couples of friends and I decided to go in on renting a shore house for the summer with twenty other people, most of whom I did not know. On Memorial Day Weekend, everyone showed up at the house and we had a party. I found myself talking with two of my new roommates, and it turned out that we had a lot in common. Late into the night we were telling stories and laughing and having a good time. Then I was asked what I do for a living. I told them that I work for the Catholic Church as a youth minister.

Then for the next two hours, I listened to both of them on the porch tell me how bad organized religion is and how unenlightened I am for being

a part of the Catholic Church. I listened as they exuded enormous amounts of energy to try to convince me that there is no God and that Jesus is fictional. I listened deep into the night and then finally said, "You know what guys, maybe someday I'll tell you what I believe, but for now, it's late and I'm pretty tired. I'm going to bed." They agreed. We went inside to find everyone already asleep. There were two spots left on the couch. The third person had to sleep on the dirty, disgusting floor.

I told them that I would take the floor, and so that's where I slept. In that one action, I hope that I showed my two new acquaintances what I believe as a member of the Church. As Gandhi said, "My life is my message." Jesus would agree.

Once all four sections are completed, post the transparency to show them what they came up with.

10:30 AM Tell each group to go back to their small groups to rewrite their respective parts of the Creed using the results of their assignment. They must work together to create a statement of belief that represents their group's reflection.

10:40 AM Conclusion

- Each group has a representative read its statement of belief.

- Point out to parents that their job is to continue to give witness to the Creed to their sons and daughters by their example. This is how to pass on our faith.

- Point out to the youth that they must continue to be open to our faith so that that may confirm it wholeheartedly when the sacrament of confirmation rolls around (or, so that one day they may fully own it as adult Christians).

10:45 AM Rehearse the ritual

10:50 AM Announcements

11:00 AM Mass

RITE OF CREED ICEBREAKER

Find a clear area of the room where people can move from one side to the other. Ask all the teens and parents to stand in the middle of the room and then give them these instructions:

> In a moment, I am going to make a series of "I believe" statements. If you agree with the statement, please move to the right side of the room. If you disagree with the statement please move to the left side of the room. If you are not sure or if "it depends," please move to the side that your belief tends to lean toward. Once you get to a side of the room for a specific statement, please seek out someone on your side to discuss why you agree or disagree. After each statement try to speak to someone new, introducing yourself each time. Any questions? Here we go!

I believe...

- dogs are better than cats
- gambling is a sin
- women should pay half on a date
- _____ is the best state in the union
- books are better than movies
- one should always make one's bed
- one should spend more than one saves
- fall is the best time of year
- *Seinfeld* is the best sitcom of all time
- jumping out of an airplane is good for one's health
- couples should only use the word "love" if they are planning to marry
- friends are just as important as family
- there is intelligent life on other planets
- the president is doing a good job

PROFESSING OUR FAITH

The term *creed* derives from the Latin *credo*, which means, "to put one's heart into something" or "to give oneself to someone or something." Professing the Creed implies commitment. The Creed is an act of praise and thanksgiving by which we confess before God and one another what God has done and is doing for us through Christ and by the power of the Holy Spirit.

There are two Creeds that are officially recognized by the Church as our profession of faith: the Apostles' Creed (not really written by the apostles but years later by the communities that they began) and the Nicene Creed.

The Nicene Creed is the one we profess each week at Mass. It was originally issued in A.D. 325 by the Council of Nicaea (present-day Turkey). Some years later, after the first ecumenical Council of Constantinople in A.D. 381, the Nicene Creed was revisited, revised, and expanded to the version we profess today.

THE NICENE CREED

We believe in one God, the Father,
the Almighty, maker of heaven and earth,
of all that is, seen and unseen.
We believe in one Lord, Jesus Christ,
the only Son of God eternally begotten of
*   the Father, God from God,*
Light from Light, true God from true God,
begotten, not made,
one in being with the Father.
Though him all things were made.
For us and for our salvation
he came down from heaven.
By the power of the Holy Spirit he was born
*   of the Virgin Mary, and became man.*
For our sake he was crucified
under Pontius Pilate;
he suffered, died, and was buried.
On the third day he rose again in fulfillment
*   of the Scriptures;*

he ascended into heaven and is seated at the
*   right hand of the Father.*
He will come again in glory to judge the
*   living and the dead,*
and his kingdom will have no end.
We believe in the Holy Spirit, the Lord,
the giver of life, who proceeds from
*   the Father and the Son.*
With the Father and the Son,
he is worshipped and glorified.
He has spoken through the prophets.
We believe in one holy catholic and
*   apostolic Church.*
We acknowledge one baptism for the
*   forgiveness of sins.*
We look for the resurrection of the dead,
and the life of the world to come.
Amen.

Nicene Creed Group 1 Assignment

We believe in one God, the Father, the Almighty, maker of heaven and earth, of all that is, seen and unseen.

Step 1: From a parent and from a youth perspective, list as many names as you can that we can attribute to God other than "Father," "Almighty," and "Creator." Explain your reasoning for each name.

Step 2: As a group, decide on two names to present to the larger group.

Step 3: Select a group member to explain your choices.

Nicene Creed Group 2 Assignment

We believe in one Lord, Jesus Christ, the only Son of God eternally begotten of the Father, God from God, Light from Light, true God from true God, begotten, not made, one in being with the Father. Through him all things were made. For us and for our salvation he came down from heaven: by the power of the Holy Spirit he was born of the Virgin Mary, and became man. For our sake he was crucified under Pontius Pilate; he suffered, died, and was buried. On the third day he rose again in fulfillment of the Scriptures; he ascended into heaven and is seated at the right hand of the Father. He will come again in glory to judge the living and the dead, and his kingdom will have no end.

To believe in the Lord Jesus is to believe in his life, death, and resurrection, the story of our salvation that is unfolded for us through the Scriptures every Sunday at Mass.

Step 1: Recalling all that you have come to know about Jesus through our Catholic tradition, list as many characteristics of Jesus as you can, both from the parent perspective and the youth perspective. Explain your answers.

Step 2: As a group, decide on two characteristics to present to the larger group.

Step 3: Select a group member to explain your choices.

Nicene Creed Group 3 Assignment

We believe in the Holy Spirit, the Lord, the giver of life, who proceeds from the Father and the Son. With the Father and the Son, he is worshipped and glorified. He has spoken through the Prophets.

To believe in the Holy Spirit is to believe that God dwells within us and is experienced in and through everything.

Step 1: From a parent and a youth perspective, list different ways in which you have experienced the Spirit of God in everyday life.

Step 2: As a group, choose two from your list to present to the larger group.

Step 3: Select a group member to explain your choices.

Nicene Creed Group 4 Assignment

We believe in one holy catholic and apostolic Church. We acknowledge one baptism for the forgiveness of sins. We look for the resurrection of the dead, and the life of the world to come. Amen.

Step 1: From a parent and from a youth perspective, list all the things that you think we the Church should be. Explain your answers.

Step 2: As a group, choose two things from your list to present to the larger group.

Step 3: Select a group member to explain your choices.

Create a transparency with the following:

We Believe in God, the:

We Believe in God's Son Who:

We Believe in the Holy Spirit Who:

We Believe in a Church Who:

THE RITE OF CREED

After the homily, the youth minister goes to the lectern and invites all the second-year candidates and their parents to gather around the altar or in front of the sanctuary.

Youth Minister My brothers and sisters, gathered with us today are our second-year confirmation candidates and their families. Through their participation in youth ministry, they are anticipating the third sacrament of initiation.

Earlier this morning, we encouraged these young people to deepen their understanding of the faith which we profess each week. They stand among us today as a sign of their openness to continue to be formed in the way of Christ.

Standing with them are their parents, their primary faith-givers. Through their continuing witness, they reveal to our candidates the Father, Son, and Holy Spirit in the ordinary events of each day.

Also present today are the leaders from our (retreat) team. These young people and adults have answered the call to share their faith in an intimate way this year with our candidates. They too will pass on our Creed through their example.

All of us here today represent the entire parish community of _____. Because of our baptism, our commitment to discipleship, all of us are responsible for one another's growing more deeply into the way of Christ.

Presider All of us promised at our baptism to be witnesses to the Creed. May we continue to be living signs of the cross, living creeds for each other, especially for our candidates. So let us all stand now together to proclaim and profess what we promise to live out each day:

All We believe in one God...

NICENE CREED RITUAL BLESSING

After the homily, the youth minister goes to the lectern and invites all the sophomores and their parents to gather around the altar or in front of the sanctuary.

Youth Minister My brothers and sisters, gathered with us today are our high school sophomores and their families. Through their participation in youth ministry, their faith continues to form.

Earlier this morning, we encouraged these young people to deepen their understanding of the faith which we profess each week. They stand among us today as a sign of their openness to continue to be formed in the way of Christ.

Standing with them are their parents, their primary faith-givers. Through their continuing witness, they reveal to our candidates the Father, Son, and Holy Spirit in the ordinary events of each day.

Also present today are the leaders from our (retreat) team. These young people and adults have answered the call to share their faith in an intimate way this year with our sophomores. They too will pass on our Creed through their example.

All of us here today represent the entire parish community of _____. Because of our baptism, our commitment to discipleship, all of us are responsible for one another's growing more deeply into the Way of Christ.

Presider All of us promised at our baptism to be witnesses to the Creed. May we continue to be living signs of the cross, living creeds for each other, especially for our young people. So let us all stand now together to proclaim and profess that which we promise to live out each day:

All We believe in one God...

 # The Rite of Covenant

Once again, we turn to Thomas Zanzig's seminal work, *Confirmed in a Faithful Community* (*Coordinators Manual*, p. 113), for guidance on this next rite for young people preparing for confirmation. (For young people already confirmed, the Rite of Covenant is replaced with a Witness Ritual Blessing. See page 109.) Zanzig suggests that we parallel the RCIA's Rite of Enrollment in order to signify the candidates' entrance into their immediate preparation for the sacrament. This is expressed ritually during a parish liturgy when the candidates sign their names in a special book designated for this yearly tradition.

A covenant in the Judeo-Christian tradition has always been accompanied by a sign. The rainbow after the great flood was the sign of the covenant between God and God's people. Then circumcision became the outward sign of this covenant. Then with Moses, the sign of the covenant became obeying the commandments, and finally Jesus said that our love for one another would be the sign of the new covenant. In an Initiation Model of Youth Ministry, the sign of this particular covenant is literally the signing of names.

The rite is not to be confused with the commitments made at confirmation. The young people make a pact with God and with the parish that they will seriously discern during the coming weeks whether or not they wish to be confirmed, and if so, what gifts they will bring to the table.

Although Zanzig's original use of this rite has the same meaning as we use it in this model, there are some differences. Namely, the Rite of Covenant in an initiation model is accompanied by a specifically designed family-based morning of reflection and most effectively takes place on the First Sunday of Lent. This is so that discernment becomes a part of their lenten journey and therefore reinforces within them and the parish the discerning and self-reflective nature of the lenten season.

RITE OF COVENANT MORNING OF REFLECTION

9:30 AM Welcome (preferably by the retreat teams that have been ministering to this age group during the year.)

    Coffee, water, and juice provided

    Bagels and muffins optional

    Distribute name tags if needed

9:40 AM Opening Prayer: Ask all to find a round table and sit at it in their family units with two or three other family units. No more than eight people per table. Light a candle in the middle or front of the room and call everyone to prayer with words such as, "Let us take some time to become aware of God's presence."

Leader The Lord is with us.

All Now and forever.

Leader Lord, open our eyes, open our ears, and open our hearts.

All And we will live your word.

Scripture

Matthew 4:1–11 (Year A)
Mark 1:12–15 (Year B)
Luke 4:1–13 (Year C)

Silent reflection

Leader Let us pray.

All Lord Jesus Christ,
you went to the desert
for forty days to discern
your ministry and mission.
There you faced
the great temptation
to deny your humanity.
But unlike Adam and Eve,
you embraced your
limited human state,
your creaturehood,
and returned to us to show us
how to be fully human.
May we too discern who we are,
embrace who we are,
and fully be who we are:
The sons and daughters of God.
We pray this in your holy name.
Amen.

9:45 AM Connect the gospel to the purpose of this morning of reflection. For example: Today is the First Sunday of Lent, and the gospel we just heard is the one we will hear at Mass. Lent begins with the story of Jesus being tempted in the desert for forty days by Satan. This temptation goes to the root of all evil (biblically speaking). The root of all evil in scripture is the denial of existence. Satan is the prince of non-being. If the biblical character named Satan had a motto, it would be: "It is better to be nothing than to be anything other than God" (recall the Garden of Eden). Why be human if you could be God? Satan tempts Jesus to deny his humanity, to deny who he is.

Likewise, *we* are perpetually tempted to deny who God made us to be. God made us to be good, very good, but would someone who is truly living in the image of God hold a grudge against anyone? Would someone who is made in the image and likeness of God fail to forgive? Would someone who is truly living in the image of God fail to serve another? Of course not, but it happens every day in every country, in every town, in every parish community, and every family.

Indeed there is not a better gospel story to begin Lent than Jesus in the desert. It is telling us to go with Jesus into the desert and find ourselves, to be who God made us to be!

And why the desert? Because there is literally nothing in the desert, and if we were to go there, our presence would become the most unique and glaring characteristic of that desert. What better place to really take a good look at ourselves than a place where there is nothing that can distract us?

This is why we are asking you to begin the Period of Discernment at the same time you begin this year's lenten journey (show the journey of faith graphic from page 35, pointing out the period of discernment). This parish is asking you to go into the desert and take a good and serious look at yourself in order to discern if confirmation is right for you. In other words, will celebrating the sacrament of confirmation make sense in light of where you are in your faith journey? And parents, guess what? You're going into the desert with them. You must help them discern, but in an honest and unselfish way.

However, before we start thinking about that,

it's important that we understand what exactly we are discerning. What is confirmation? What has it come to mean in this day and age?

9:50 AM Discerning confirmation

Introduction: As Msgr. James B. Songy writes: "The theology of the sacrament of confirmation is rather vague, especially when it separates from the other 'sacraments of initiation,' namely baptism and Eucharist. To some it represents the maturing of an individual in the faith; to others it is the personal commitment of the individual to active membership in the faith; to others it is the personal ratification or acceptance of the commitment made by one's parents at baptism; for others it represents the so-called 'baptism in the Spirit'" (Songy, *Questions & Answers for Catholics*, p. 82).

Through our lived experience of sacramental ministry, we have come to the realization that confirmation is all of these things.

Confirmation...

» *Confirms baptism*

Ask all the parents at each table to describe to the rest of their table in detail what they remember about their teens' baptism. After you have given them a chance to describe, explain the following:

> When we were baptized, our parents and our godparents made a commitment to raise us in such a way that our lives would reflect the life of Christ. They brought out the divine goodness in us through their parenthood. In and through the sacrament of confirmation, we confirm this commitment and assume full responsibility for living out the call to be the presence of Christ in our world today.

» *Completes the sacraments of initiation*

Take a volunteer from the group (preferably the "group clown" or someone who is not easily embarrassed and loves the spotlight). Say to everyone, "When we first begin our initiation process, we enter into the waters of baptism (pour a cup of water on volunteer's head), and we are given new life in Christ. We put on Christ, if you will, and wear him like a cloak. (Put white robe on volunteer.) Then the initiation process continues when we confirm this new reality which is sealed by the Holy Spirit (rub scented oil on volunteer's forehead). Finally, the initiation process is brought to fullness when we share in the Eucharist, the Lord's Supper (unveil a giant loaf of bread and a pitcher of wine and gesture to the volunteer as if you expect him/her to eat and drink it all, stopping him/her just before he/she attempts)." You might want to arrange for a volunteer in secret before the meeting. Proceed to explain the following:

> The sacraments of initiation are baptism, confirmation and Eucharist (in that order). Originally in our Christian tradition, these sacraments were celebrated together at one time by young adults and adults who "came to believe." This part of our tradition has been changed in the Western Church. The three sacraments of initiation have been separated; consequently, confirmation for most dioceses is celebrated after first Eucharist. Since this is currently the tradition of our diocese, confirmation is the completion of the sacraments of initiation. In other words, once one is confirmed in our diocese, one has full membership in the faith community. However, our celebration of Eucharist (Mass) is the culmination of all sacraments and brings us all to fullness or "completion." It should also be noted that the original tradition of celebrating all three sacraments together in the proper order is the norm for adult converts participating in the RCIA process and for young people in the children's catechumenate.

» *Bestows upon us the Gift of the Holy Spirit*

> Fr. Michael Himes, a noted speaker and professor of theology at Boston College, theologizes that "a sacrament recognizes, acknowledges, and celebrates that which has always been the case sometime,

somewhere." In and through the sacrament of confirmation, one formally (at long last) recognizes, acknowledges, and celebrates the fact that one has been gifted by the Holy Spirit one's whole life. So, it is not that the Holy Spirit "all of a sudden" appears at confirmation. Rather, it is we who "all of a sudden" recognize, acknowledge, and celebrate the gift of the ever-present Spirit in our midst. One place where it can be rather easy to recognize the Holy Spirit or the Advocate is within our families. Our parents have been and will continue to be our advocates or encouragers. The Holy Spirit is alive through them. Their example helps us recognize the encouraging Spirit in the midst of our parish community as well.

After explaining, ask the parents at each table to once again share with the teens what they remember about their own confirmation. How was it different? Do they remember memorizing the seven gifts of the Holy Spirit, for example?

» Is a Commitment to Embrace Christianity

Christianity is our faith. It is who we are. Confirmation is a commitment to love the way Jesus, the Bread of Life, loved.

After explaining, ask that each teen share with their table one thing that they really like about being a follower of Jesus. What do they like about it?

» Is a Commitment to Accept and Practice Roman Catholicism

Roman Catholicism is the tradition through which we choose to express who we are. Thus, confirmation is a commitment to recognize, acknowledge, and celebrate who we are in and through the Roman Catholic religious tradition.

After explaining, ask everyone (parents and teens) to share with their table one thing that they really like about the Roman Catholic religious tradition.

» Is a Commitment to Share the Gift of Ourselves with Our Parish Family

Ask for ten youth volunteers to stand. One by one, ask them to name one way in which they see themselves staying involved in the parish once they are confirmed. Then proceed to explain the following:

We, the Church, believe that all of us make up the Body of Christ. As a parish community, we believe that when we gather around the table (the altar), we do not gather as individuals as one would gather at a ball game, but rather, we gather as one body. We commit to share life with one another in order to build up the Body of Christ. When one of us is missing, we are incomplete. Confirmation is a commitment to embrace this belief.

» Is a Beginning

In our highly academic society, it is easy for us to mistake confirmation as a "graduation from the parish." It is very tempting for us to see it as an end. But confirmation is a beginning. Newly confirmed individuals can be likened to rookies in the Major League. There is still more to learn. Confirmation marks the beginning of a new chapter in one's faith journey.

10:20 AM Conclusion (brief restatement of purpose of the morning's reflection, questions, comments, etc.)

10:30 AM Confirmation name and sponsor review (see Appendix L)

10:40 AM   **Rehearse rite of covenant** explaining the relevance of the gestures

10:50 AM   **Final interview scheduling** (see Appendix D)

11:00 AM   **Mass** (rite of covenant)

RITE OF COVENANT (AFTER HOMILY)

Candidates are pre-seated, either together or with their families.

Youth Minister My brothers and sisters, these candidates who celebrate with us today are completing their period of preparation and entering their period of discernment. They have heard the Word of God and they have acted on the Word of God. They have recognized the Lord on their journey through the sharing of themselves. I present them to this community as candidates who are sufficiently prepared to be enrolled among the elect for their future celebration of confirmation.

Presider I invite our parents of the candidates, our catechists, and the (sophomore retreat) team to stand. (*Pause*) You have been and will continue to be witnesses of the gospel for these young people. And so I ask you: Have these candidates fully listened to God's Word proclaimed by the Church?

Parents, Catechists, Leaders They have.

Presider Have they responded to that Word and begun to walk with an awareness of God's presence within and around them?

Parents, Catechists, Leaders They have.

Presider Have they shared the company of their Christian brothers and sisters and joined with them in prayer, worship, and loving service?

Parents, Catechists, Leaders They have.

Presider You may be seated. And now I speak to all present in this assembly: Are you ready to support the testimony expressed about these candidates and include them in your prayer and affection as they move on in their journey toward the sacrament of confirmation?

All We are.

Presider Finally, I ask our second-year candidates to please stand. (Pause) Your parents, catechists, peer leaders, and this entire community have spoken in your favor. The Church in the name of Christ accepts their judgment and calls you to confirmation. Since you have already heard the call of Christ, you must now express your response to that call clearly and in the presence of the whole Church. And so I ask: Do you wish to enter fully into the immediate preparation for the sacrament of confirmation?

Candidates We do.

Presider I invite you then to offer your names for enrollment.

Candidates come forward, sign their names into the book, and remain in or near the sanctuary.

Presider On behalf of our entire parish community, I now invite you into the immediate preparation for the sacrament of confirmation. May your discernment be Spirit-filled.

All Thanks be to God.

Witness Ritual Blessing

If a senior high youth ministry consists of young people who were confirmed in junior high or earlier, a witness ritual blessing can be implemented in order to acknowledge the next step in the adolescent faith journey (the do you believe? stage). At this point in the faith journey, young people are invited through a ritual blessing to try to describe the current state of their faith and how their lives are affected by it (witness). Like the Rite of Covenant, it serves as a sign that the young people are willing to enter into serious reflection on whether their faith experiences have prepared them for an "owned" faith. As a means to express this reality, the young people are invited to give a brief testimony of their faith.

This ritual blessing will be most enriching if it takes place after one has experienced all eight components of youth ministry for at least a year and a half (this includes a full weekend encounter retreat, service opportunities, and all the previously mentioned ritual blessings). If we are asking the young people to reflect on their preparedness for an owned faith, they must have sufficient experience on which to reflect. A year and a half of participation in total parish youth ministry can provide sufficient experience (although more time

may be needed for some).

Lent is the recommended time of year to do this ritual blessing because of its reflective and discerning nature. It is also recommended that many witness ritual blessings be scheduled throughout Lent at the different parish weekend Masses, with no more than four young people giving witness at any one Mass (this particular ritual can take much longer than the previously described rituals if many youth are scheduled at the same Mass). However, one family-based morning, afternoon, or evening of reflection for all involved will suffice and can be scheduled on the first Sunday of Lent in order to prepare for the ritual blessings that will follow.

Note: The young person's openness and desire to participate in any ritual blessing is necessary, especially in this case. Those who have absolutely no idea how to answer the reflection questions on the worksheet will not find this ritual or the preparation for it helpful (one would expect that anyone who has participated in all eight components of youth ministry will not have this problem, but one never knows). It is for this reason that the Witness Ritual Blessing and family-based reflection not be designated to only one age group (i.e. sophomores), but be an option for all upperclassers whenever they feel called to it. Expect the numbers to be very small at first, but to grow after a couple of years of practice.

See Appendix M for an example of a young person's witness.

WITNESS RITUAL BLESSING REFLECTION

9:30 AM Welcome (preferably by the retreat teams that have been ministering to this age group during the year.)

> Coffee, water, and juice provided
> Bagels and muffins optional
> Distribute name tags if needed

9:40 AM Opening Prayer Ask all to find a round table and sit at it in their family units with two or three other family units. No more than eight people per table. Light a candle in the middle or front of the room and call everyone to prayer with words such as, "Let us take some time to become aware of God's presence."

> **Leader** The Lord is with us.
>
> **All** Now and forever.
>
> **Leader** Lord, open our eyes, open our ears, and open our hearts.
>
> **All** And we will live your word.

Scripture

> Matthew 4:1–11 (Year A)
> Mark 1:12–15 (Year B)
> Luke 4:1–13 (Year C)

(Silent reflection)

> **Leader** Let us pray.
>
> **All** Lord Jesus Christ,
> You went to the desert
> for forty days to discern
> your ministry and mission.
> There you faced

the great temptation
to deny your humanity.
But unlike Adam and Eve,
you embraced your
limited human state,
your creaturehood,
and returned to us as a witness
to what it means to be fully human.
May we too discern who we are,
embrace who we are,
and fully be who we are:
The sons and daughters of God
and witnesses to the whole world.
We pray this in your holy name.
Amen.

9:45 AM Connect the gospel to the purpose of this morning of reflection. For example: Today is the First Sunday of Lent, and the gospel we have just heard is the one we will hear at Mass. Lent begins with the story of Jesus being tempted in the desert for forty days by Satan. This temptation goes to the root of all evil (biblically speaking). The root of all evil in scripture is the denial of existence. Satan is the prince of non-being. If the biblical character named Satan had a motto, it would be: "It is better to be nothing than to be anything other than God" (recall the Garden of Eden). Why be human if you could be God? Satan tempts Jesus to deny his humanity, to deny who he is.

Likewise, *we* are perpetually tempted to deny who God made us to be. God made us to be good, very good, but would someone who is truly living in the image of God hold a grudge against anyone? Would someone who is made in the image and likeness of God fail to forgive? Would someone who is truly living in the image of God fail to serve another? Of course not, but it happens every day in every country, in every town, in every parish community, and every family.

Indeed there is no better gospel story to begin Lent than Jesus in the desert. It is telling us to go with Jesus into the desert and find ourselves, to be who God made us to be!

And why the desert? Because there is literally nothing in the desert, and if we were to go there, our presence would become the most unique and glaring characteristic of that desert. What better place to really take a good look at ourselves than in the desert where there is nothing that can distract us?

This is why we are inviting you to think about how you might give witness to your faith while you begin this year's lenten journey (show the journey of faith graphic from page 42, pointing out the Do You Believe? stage). This parish is inviting you to go into the desert and take a good and serious look at yourself in order to discern how your membership in the Christian community and the Catholic Church makes sense for you. We are inviting you to once again look within yourself and ask, "Do I believe?" And parents, guess what? You're going into the desert with them. You must help them discern, but in an honest and unselfish way.

Today's reflection is the beginning of that process.

9:50 AM In order to get the ball rolling, ask the parents to share with the people at their tables some things about their own faith. Here are some examples of discussion questions:

- How is your faith different now than it was when you were a teenager?

- In what ways do you think of God differently now than you did back then?

- At what point in your life did your faith definitely become your own?

- In what ways does your faith affect your decisions in life?

10:00 AM Explain the following: What the parents at each table just did was give witness to their faith, and through doing so, we heard examples of owned faith. An owned faith can have many different levels, but the common thread is that people who own their faith are aware that God is intimately connected to their whole being. They believe in God, not because others tell them to, but because of this internal and external awareness. The Witness Ritual Blessing for which we are preparing is an opportunity for you to share with our community how you have been and are becoming aware of God in your everyday life. It will be a sign that your faith is becoming your own.

10:05 AM Example Witness: Prior to this reflection, a few upperclassers who perhaps gave excellent witness talks a year before, are asked to give them again at this gathering (updated if need be).

10:15 AM Invite the young people at each table to take ten minutes on their own to jot down their thoughts on the handout. Invite parents to gather around the food and beverage table in order to give their teens some privacy.

10:25 AM Parents rejoin the tables. Invite the young people to share the thoughts that they jotted down with the people at their table. Encourage them to try to explain their thoughts, even if it is very difficult to do so. Encourage parents to listen and ask questions. This is an important step in self actualization and is usually not an easy one. It may take some time to find the right words.

10:50 AM Explain the following: The next step is up to you. Throughout the season of Lent, you will have an opportunity to give your ten sentence or less witness to our parish community at one of the weekend Masses. It will be a sign that you are moving closer to a faith that is your own. If you believe that you are ready for this step now, you can sign up before you leave today for one the Masses in the coming weeks. If you need time to reflect, that's fine. Just let us know when you are ready, even if that means a year or two from now.

Also, know that this is not required in any sense of the word. It is something that will only help you in your faith journey if you *want* to do it. Once you sign up for the Witness Ritual Blessing, you will be asked to meet with (one of the adult catechists, one of the priests, the youth minister, etc.) for a one-on-one conversation about what you want to say. It's just one more way to help you find the right words. Before the homily, you will be called by name to come to the lectern in order to give your witness. You will stay in the sanctuary until all have given witness, then the priest will lead the community in a blessing over you. You return to your seat, probably to some applause, and Mass will continue with the priest's homily. Any questions? (Hopefully the presiding priest will be able to speak about some of the substance of the witness talks in his homily and relate it to the readings.)

11:00 AM Conclude with a short prayer of your choice.

WITNESS RITUAL BLESSING WORKSHEET

Name one or more experiences that have made a profound difference in your faith.

What aspects of our faith and religion (if any) did you have or are you still having trouble accepting or believing and how did you/can you come to accept and believe in them?

If you wanted to tell someone about your Christian faith and Roman Catholic religious tradition, what might you say?

Use your previous answers to help formulate your answer to the following question. This will be your witness. It is to be no longer than ten sentences and is for you to work on at home.

At this moment in my life, I choose to be a Catholic Christian because...

WITNESS RITUAL BLESSING

Immediately following the gospel.

Presider My brothers and sisters, during this season of Lent, we are invited to journey within ourselves in order to discover a faith that is ever-forming and ever-deepening. We look to Jesus as the ultimate example of what it means to live by faith. Today, our young brother(s)/sister(s) (*names*) have come forward to give public witness to their own awareness of faith and how they are choosing to live by it in the way of Christ.

Young people come forward and give their witness talks. When all are completed they move together to the center aisle and stand before the altar. The presider invites the whole assembly to stand and extend their arms in blessing.

All Loving God,
we thank you
for our young parishioners,
without whom we are incomplete.
Bless them
as they move ever closer
to an adult faith.
May *their* witness to the gospel
be written on *our* hearts
and reveal to us
the presence of *your* Spirit
who lives and dwells
within this community of faith.
Open them to your wisdom
to continue to seek you
in all experiences and relationships
and grant us the fortitude and understanding
to join them, as together
we answer the call of Christian discipleship
today and every day.
We ask this through Christ our Lord.
Amen.

Young people return to their seats, and the priest gives the homily.

The Rite of Confirmation

Much has been written and said concerning the sacrament of confirmation. There is still much controversy surrounding this rite, especially concerning the appropriate age of those to be confirmed as well as the appropriate order of the three sacraments of initiation. Since this section is written for parishes who celebrate confirmation during the high school years, we need not worry ourselves with this controversy and simply deal with the situation at hand.

Within this model of youth ministry, the rite of confirmation is first and foremost a celebration. It marks the end of the Period of Discernment and the beginning of the Period of Celebration. Everything that has to do with this rite should be celebratory in nature. For example, the traditional confirmation rehearsal which usually takes place the night before the ritual, should be festive, at least at the onset.

One effective practice has been to have all the upperclassers who were the candidates' retreat team leaders during the previous year stand at the doors of the church and enthusiastically greet them, their families, and their sponsors as they enter the building for rehearsal. Another effective practice is to begin the rehearsal by having everyone sing the opening song scheduled for the confirmation Mass and to keep singing it until everyone sings it with spirit. These types of things set a celebratory tone right away.

Next, the rite of confirmation should be celebrated consciously, meaning that everyone involved should have a basic understanding of the history and symbolism of the ritual actions. For this reason, the confirmation rehearsal should be publicized as a confirmation reflection/rehearsal. Candidates, sponsors, and parents should not only rehearse the ritual, but should also be catechized about it and have the opportunity to reflect on it as they walk through it.

THE OFFICIAL DOCUMENT

In the official Church document entitled *The Rite of Confirmation*, the introduction stipulates that not only the rite itself should take place during a eucharistic celebration, but that "all the people of God, represented by the families and friends of the candidates and by members of the local community, will be invited to take part in such a celebration" (no. 4). For this reason, it is recommended that the rite take place at a regular Sunday parish Mass (or Saturday vigil Mass) in order to acknowledge the community's on-going role in initiating its members. Furthermore, even though no directive is given in the ritual itself concerning liturgical time or seasons, it is recommended that the rite be scheduled during the Easter season up to and including Pentecost. This not only provides consistency with the spirit of the early Church, but enables the parish community to truly use the liturgical calendar as an initiation journey from life with Christ to death with Christ to new life in Christ.

In an Initiation Model of Youth Ministry, there is no timetable for confirmation. It is celebrated when one discerns "readiness." It is possible for one to remain in the Period of Discernment for months or years. This is especially important when the sacramental theology of confirmation is coupled with the developmental reality of an intentional faith. In other words, if indeed it is the decision of the parish to present the sacrament as a declaration of an owned faith, confirmation should not be celebrated by anyone who is not ready to acknowledge that his/her faith is intentional.

As another option, a parish may decide that it is not necessary for their candidates to have an awareness of an owned faith in order to be confirmed (which is completely orthodox), and choose to incorporate the Intentional Faith Ritual Blessing in the later post-confirmation stages of senior high youth ministry.

This book recommends that as long as confirmation is celebrated in senior high, the awareness of an intentional faith should be part of one's decision to be confirmed, whether with one's classmates or later in life.

RITE OF CONFIRMATION REFLECTION/ REHEARSAL

To be scheduled in the church building no more than two days before the ritual. Invite candidates, their sponsors, and their parents.

7:00 PM Gather in the church. Retreat team leaders greet everyone outside the front doors with enthusiasm (applause, cheering, high fives, backslaps, hugs if appropriate, etc.)

7:10 PM Arrange candidates, sponsors and parents into the seating assignments for the ritual.

- When situated ask all to stand up and introduce themselves to everyone seated around them.
- Introduce yourself and any other leaders present.
- Ask all to open their hymnals to whatever the opening song is going to be at the rite of confirmation. Sing the song together. Encourage all to sing with spirit. You may need to enlist the help of the music minister or someone who can play the piano, organ, or guitar.

7:20 PM Opening prayer

Leader In the name of the Father, and of the Son, and of the Holy Spirit.

All Amen.

Leader Lord, as we gather this evening
to reflect on the sacrament of
confirmation,
we call upon your Spirit to
open our minds
so that we may hear and comprehend
the truth of your Word.
We ask that you help us to
open our mouths
So that we may proclaim
the Good News of Jesus Christ
through our words and actions,
and we ask that you open our hearts
so that our lives may be a
continuation of the gospel.
We ask this through Christ our Lord.

All Amen.

Scripture Proclaim the gospel reading that will be proclaimed at the rite of confirmation Mass.

Reflection Say in your own words: "I have a question for each person here. Parents: What do you hear in this gospel that says something about your role as a parent? Sponsors: What do you hear in this gospel that says something about your role as sponsor? And candidates: what do you hear in this gospel that says something about your role as a newly confirmed member of our parish? Now, this is not a test question. I am not looking for you to come up with "the right answer." I am simply asking you to reflect on what this gospel is saying to you in light of the sacrament of confirmation. The gospel will be proclaimed one more time, so if you were not listening before, you can listen up now! After we hear the gospel again, candidates share your thoughts with your sponsors and sponsors share your thoughts back. Parents, share your thoughts with one another or with whomever is sitting next to you."

Scripture Re-proclaim the gospel.

Sharing Allow five to eight minutes

7:40 PM Large group feedback: Are there any interesting thoughts from your reflection that you felt the large group would benefit from hearing?

7:50 PM Rite of confirmation rehearsal: Each diocese will have guidelines for the ritual that are to be followed here. As the ritual is rehearsed, an explanation of the symbolism and history of the ritual actions should be conveyed. *The Apostolic Constitution on the Sacrament of Confirmation* and the *Catechism of the Catholic Church* are two primary sources that can be used to prepare your notes.

8:20 PM Questions and announcements

8:30 PM Closing prayer

Intentional Faith Ritual Blessing

An intentional faith is what Robert Duggan describes as "committed belonging" ("Parish as a Center...", p. 21). It means that one's membership in the Church is primarily based on an intentional decision to live as a disciple of Christ (one who carries on the mission of Jesus). As we have learned, one is developmentally incapable of having a full awareness of faith until late adolescence, and therefore any fully intentional decision to live by faith cannot be made until one has reached this stage of development.

As a means to acknowledge the reality of an intentional faith, the parish can incorporate into its youth ministry a ritual blessing preceded by a day of renewal that gives young people the opportunity to express an awareness of their own intentional faith; that is, to declare once and for all that their membership in the parish and the Church at large is defined primarily in terms of "committed belonging." Simply put: "It is no longer my faith solely because my parents chose it for me, but because I choose it for myself as well."

This ritual blessing is primarily designed for parishes who celebrate confirmation before the high school years; however, as suggested earlier, some parishes that confirm early on in senior

high may find that this ritual blessing affords upperclassers an opportunity to express an intentional faith that simply was developmentally impossible when they were confirmed.

I recommend that the Intentional Faith Ritual Blessing be scheduled sometime during the Easter season. Easter and baptism go hand in hand, and this ritual blessing cannot be disconnected from baptism. An awareness of an intentional faith is, after all, a sign that the grace poured out in baptism continues to flow in our lives and continues to bring us to wholeness.

THE SPRINKLING RITE

The ritual blessing takes place as a part of the sprinkling rite. After the water is blessed and before the people are sprinkled, the young people bless themselves from the font as a sign that their faith has become their own. Then they assist the presider in the sprinkling as a sign that they are now fully prepared and fully willing to pass their faith on to others. (Notice that this is the first ritual blessing where the young people bless *themselves*, and the ritual of sprinkling is an outward sign in contrast to the inward signs expressed during the previous rituals. Baptism calls us to go out into the world and spread the Good News, and an owned faith allows us to have full awareness of this mission.)

The day of renewal should take place on the same day as the ritual blessing (perhaps a Saturday with the ritual blessing scheduled at the Vigil Mass). It can take on many forms; therefore this book will not lay out a step-by-step plan for a day of renewal as it does for the previously described mornings of reflection. We will, however, make the following suggestions as to what can be included in a day of renewal:

- A leadership team consisting of adults and upperclassers who have previously participated in the Intentional Faith Ritual Blessing. The team is trained to lead the day of renewal.

- Icebreaker

- Witness talks around the theme of "owned faith." See Appendix N for an outline of one such talk.

- Small group discussions

- Large group prayer service

- Large group activity

- Question and answer session

- Lunch and snack breaks

- Viewing of video or PowerPoint presentation with discussion

- Ritual Blessing rehearsal

- Parish Mass that includes the Intentional Faith Ritual Blessing

- A dinner reception after Mass with parents and members of the parish

Depending on preference, parents may or may not be invited to participate in the whole day's schedule. (My preference is to invite parents to participate in a portion of the day that addresses the reality of their teens' movement from a "faith given" to a "faith owned.")

INTENTIONAL FAITH RITUAL BLESSING

Call to Worship

Youth Minister — Good morning/evening. Welcome to _____. (*pause*) The gospel calls us to intentionally live our lives in the way of Christ. Our baptism challenges us and unites us through the power of the Holy Spirit to live as members of Christ's Body, the Church. Today we will celebrate a simple yet profound ritual blessing in which our young people will acknowledge that they have come to a full awareness of the implications of their baptismal promises. Blessing themselves with the holy water from the font expresses their intention to remember their baptism and remain open to God's grace as they continue their lifelong journey from a "faith given" to a "faith owned." May their presence be a reminder of God's continued strength and may their participation in the sprinkling rite deepen our own baptismal call to be living water to all those who thirst. Let us rise as an Easter people and together gather our hearts and minds into one body, as we begin our great celebration of who we are!

Entrance song and greeting

Presider — My brothers and sisters, today we are challenged by the gospel to (*insert appropriate wording for the Mass of the day*). We also welcome today our young brothers and sisters (*say their names if time allows*) who have come forward to express their intentional faith. I invite them now to join me at the baptismal font.

Young people and presider [and concelebrants/deacon if present] gather around the font. The presider begins the sprinkling rite, using choice C from the Sacramentary for the blessing of the water.

Presider   Young disciples, the first time you stood at the font, your parents and godparents held you. Now you stand on your own, open to take on the responsibilities of an adult faith. We invite you to bless yourselves from the font as a sign that your faith is intentional and to share in the sprinkling as a sign that your inner conversion has deepened your awareness of spreading the gospel through your witness.

Young people bless themselves from the font. Each then receives a branch or spurge and sprinkles different sections of the assembly. Music may accompany the sprinkling. After the sprinkling, the young people return to their seats. The presider returns to his place and prays the concluding prayer to the sprinkling rite (see Sacramentary).

CONCLUSION

THE OTHER
NINETY PERCENT!

Sally seemed to be the perfect candidate for the job. She had a Masters in Religious Education. She had a recommendation from a bishop and experience in a diocesan youth ministry office. When the parish interviewed her, she really knew her stuff. She understood how to give youth ministry a structure and was familiar with the different models out there. Compared to all the other candidates for the youth minister position, on paper she was the best. Sally was hired because everyone on the search committee was really impressed with her credentials.

The parish had already established a fairly strong retreat process and outreach program for youth, so Sally did not really need to start from scratch. She delved right in to what was already established, but after a couple of retreat team meetings and service trips to the soup kitchen, it became obvious to everyone involved that Sally had very poor relational skills. In other words, she was unable to relate to the young people, their parents, and the other adults involved. For whatever reason, she just could not speak their language.

Unfortunately, this resulted in the young people making fun of her behind her back and the parents and other adults eventually losing respect for her. No matter how much the staff tried helping her to be more relational, she simply did not have it in her. She lasted a year and a half, but the pastor had to tell her that he could not renew her contract.

The irony of this whole book is that you could follow all of its suggestions on vision and strategy, but unless the people involved in your youth ministry are relational, this book will not help you. In other words, the three goals of youth ministry will not even come close to being reached if relational ministry is not front and center.

RELATIONAL MINISTRY

In my view, relational ministry in the Church is encapsulated in the story of the coming of the Spirit (Acts 2:1–13). The Spirit of God filled the members of the early Church and enabled them to proclaim in many different languages. This is not only the birth of the Church, but the birth of the relational minister within the Church. One must be able to speak the language before one can be an effective minister.

Sally spoke English, of course, but did not speak the language of the youth, or their parents, or their catechists. Her credentials in the end meant very little because she was unable to establish a mutually respectful relationship in her ministry. Does this mean that Sally is an awful person? No, of course not. It simply means that Sally needs to find a venue where she speaks the language (for her sake and the church's sake).

Show me a parish that is getting good results in youth ministry, and I'll show you a parish that stresses relationships over everything else. Even those parishes that lack a youth ministry vision can still see a good amount of short-term success if the ministry is relational (of course, in those parishes, youth ministry tends to fizzle out when the relational minister leaves: "Without a vision, the people perish" [Proverbs 29:18]).

In a sense, this book assumes that your parish already takes a "relational ministry" approach in all that it does. It assumes that the leadership in youth ministry not only can relate but also assumes that it empowers others to be in true relationship. This is really ninety percent of all ministry.

As the pastoral staff could not teach Sally how to be relational, this book cannot teach you to relate to youth and their families. You either have it or you don't. But once a parish has relational youth ministry established, it becomes vital to work on the other ten percent, which is vision and strategy. Exactly what this book is all about.

The U.S. bishops have given us an excellent vision of youth ministry that challenges parishes to go beyond schooling, "confirmation class," and/ or "youth group," in order to incorporate eight components that help form the whole person. The RCIA and family-based faith formation processes have given us a strategy that not only connects us to the early Church and the way that they "made disciples," but empowers parents and gives them the tools needed to live out their role as the primary faith givers.

AN EYE ON THE PRIZE

An Initiation Model of Youth Ministry as outlined in this book is a strategy on how to do parish senior high youth ministry that keeps its eye on the prize (*Renewing the Vision*) and uses every resource at its disposal to get there. It is not perfect, but many have found it to be the "least inadequate." With Eucharist at its center (Eucharist is all about relationship), an Initiation Model of Youth Ministry is structured in such a way that all eight components can be experienced through intergenerational and age-appropriate opportunities. It is through this participation in the total life of the parish that the adolescent faith continues to be formed. Therefore, it becomes important to stop every once in while along the way to recognize, acknowledge, and celebrate the different stages of faith growth through rites or ritual blessings.

Overall, this book speaks of a new wine and a new wine skin. As the gospel points out, one cannot put new wine into an old wineskin or the skin will burst and make a mess. One must use a new wineskin to hold the new wine (Matthew 9:17, Mark 2:22, Luke 5:37–38). Initiation theology and family-based faith formation within the scope of *Renewing the Vision* is the new wine, and an Initiation Model of Youth Ministry is the new wineskin that works for the following reasons:

- **It is about parish youth ministry, not a youth program.** Youth ministry is an integral part of the life of the parish and not a separate program connected to the parish in name only. It shares a common vision with all other ministries in the parish. The DRE, the youth ministry coordinator, and/or catechists are not the only people who minister to and with young people. Everyone in the parish is a youth minister (whether they know it or not).

- **It is about educating religiously, not just religious education.** Religious education (or catechesis) is only a small part of youth ministry. True comprehensive youth ministry and holistic faith formation are realized as a result of equally stressing all eight components of youth ministry, the religious experiences within the total life of the parish and beyond *is* the education or curriculum.

- **It is about flowing with the rest of the universal Church through the Lectionary cycle, not about depending on a textbook to determine the structure.** No matter how well written a textbook may be, when basing youth ministry on it, it disconnects youth from the rest of the parish and the Church at large. The life of the parish flows with the liturgical cycle, and therefore so too does youth ministry.

- **It is about participating in the parish, not about doing the requirements.** It is assumed that *all* baptized members of a parish will share their time and talent in some way with the community, not out of obligation or even a desire to help out, but because it is who we profess to be.

- **It is about celebrating sacraments like Eucharist and confirmation, not receiving them.** This is not just about semantics. It's about attitude. It is about celebrating who we are because as St. Augustine said, "It is ourselves that we place on the altar." One gets out of a sacrament whatever one puts into it.

- **It is about parents actively participating, not just helping out when asked.** Parents participate in youth ministry *with* their teens and are nourished and formed just as much as their children. They do not view themselves as mere chaperones fulfilling a duty, but as disciples answering a call. Parents continue to do what they promised to do at their child's baptism: make a disciple. Youth ministry provides a good venue.

- **It is about wanting to go to Mass, not having to go to Mass.** When Mass is done well, youth and their families will want to participate. There is no need for guilt trips or manipulative techniques. Feed them with bland rice cakes and they'll have no enthusiasm for it. Feed them with cotton candy, and they will eventually get sick of it. Feed them with wonderful meals, and they will be back for more.

- **It is about intergenerational experiences, not "youth only" experiences.** Intergenerational youth ministry can be more than just a nice thought when a deliberate effort is made to incorporate youth and their families into the life of the parish.

- **It's about age-appropriate opportunities, not a "one size fits all" program.** The physical, emotional, psychological, social, and spiritual differences between fourteen-year-olds and eighteen-year-olds have more developmental disparities than any other four-year span in the human life cycle. Youth ministry programming is structured with this reality in mind.

- **It is about empowering youth and adults, not keeping youth busy until they graduate or (even worse) are confirmed.** Parents are empowered by being given the opportunity and tools they need to share their faith with their teens. Young people are empowered by a community who values their presence and calls them to authentic discipleship.

- **It is about fostering faith development and maturity, not keeping the adolescent faith adolescent.** As the U.S. bishops write: "Educated Christians who have not grown beyond an adolescent level of faith development are limited in their ability to achieve personal integration and to make a contribution to society" (*Empowered by*

the Spirit, #53). It's about "fostering the total personal and spiritual growth of each young person" so they will be able to own the faith when they reach young adulthood.

- **It is about, "Ask not what my parish can do for me, ask what I can do for my parish."** It's about finding God within ourselves and others through the parish. As one young person once said when asked to sum up the New Testament, "It's basically about being selfless, not selfish. If we are selfless, we experience God. If we are selfish, we do not." Amen!

So that's my take on parish senior high youth ministry. And it works.

It may take some courage on the part of the parish to implement many of the suggestions in this book. There is certainly a large degree of "letting go" and trusting in the Holy Spirit that has to take place in order for initiation theology to take root. For some, it will require a huge paradigm shift. For others it may require a simple tweaking of attitude (which often requires a change in semantics). Whatever the case, I hope that you, the reader, have been nourished and are more eager than ever to minister to, with, by, and for your youth and their families!

Case Studies

The following case studies are based on some of my experiences in youth ministry (with some hyperbole, but amazingly, not much). I invite you to apply the principles laid out in this book when thinking about how you might respond to each scenario.

Each case study is a good tool for personal reflection as well as for discussion groups (youth ministry teams, youth minister support groups, staff meetings, etc.). If used as a topic of discussion, remember to respect differing points of view; however, I invite your group to try to apply initiation theology to the analysis, and to try to find consensus (remember, consensus does not mean "compromise," it means "finding an analysis that everyone can agree as being accurate.")

GOOD LITURGY?

Before the diocesan youth rally closing liturgy began, the youth minister/leader of song tried to get everyone pumped up for Mass by starting the wave in the outdoor arena. Naturally, the mostly youth assembly readily obliged.

The opening song began: "Oh God, I want to know you. I want you in my life. You are so awesome, with me in my strife. I was down and you were there. You lifted me up, up in the air. It's me and God, God and me. There is no other way to be," sang the group of highly energized teenagers. As they sang, they used hand gestures corresponding to each word. In fact, just about every song sung at the liturgy was accompanied by some kind of hand and body gestures led by the youth music group who called themselves "In Your Face with Christ."

The thirty-minute homily, given by the bishop, consisted mostly of pleas to the crowd to cheer because Jesus loves us and because we are Catholic. He never mentioned the readings. It was the Easter season, but no baptismal font was present. The Glory to God and the Creed were skipped (too long). There were youth lectors and ministers of communion, all trained for the first time one hour before the liturgy began.

Mass ended and half the young people were asking themselves, "Why can't Mass in our parish be like this?" The other half were saying, "That was really weird."

- *What concerns you the most about the liturgy described above?*

- *How might you disagree with the concern (or lack of concern) of others?*

- *What role, if any, do you think "Praise Music" and/or "Christian Rock" should have in our Catholic liturgies?*

- *What do you think might be some of the factors that led to half the assembly wanting more liturgies like this at home and the other half leaving confused?*

BREAK THE ICE, NOT THE WILL

Joey had just begun freshman year of high school. He was in a new school and his parents switched to a new parish because they felt that it had "better youth ministry." Joey was a good kid, but not the outgoing type, at least not until he felt comfortable within a group.

It was the first youth ministry event of the year and the first of Joey's life. He entered the parish center with an almost unbearably enthusiastic greeting from a group of hugging and singing upperclassers he had never met before. "Hey, what's your name?" they asked him.

"Joey."

"Joey, come here." A bubbly girl wrapped a blindfold around his head and said, "Now you have to crawl around on the floor making a donkey noise until you find the other person in the room making a donkey noise. Go!!"

Somewhat in shock, Joey reluctantly got down on his knees and semi-hee-hawed into the room. After ten seconds, he stopped and began to stand up and take off his blindfold. "Hey, get back on the floor, that's cheating!" yelled one of the kids leading the activity.

Joey responded, "I have to go to the bathroom," and walked out of the room. He thought to himself, "I'd rather be anywhere but here."

- *How much time and attention does your youth ministry put into planning icebreakers?*

- *What might have been some of the causes that led to the choice of an inappropriate icebreaker for the previously described event?*

- *How do you balance the empowering of young people to be involved in youth ministry programming decisions with the desire and expectation to be professional?*

- *What types of icebreakers would you recommend for the first moments of the first youth ministry event during one's first year of senior high youth ministry?*

A PLACE TO HANG OUT OR A PLACE TO BE FORMED?

The phone rings in the afternoon as you're preparing for a retreat team meeting that is going to take place later in the evening. You answer:

"Youth ministry, can I help you?"

"Yes, hi, Fred. This is Gina Jones from the Women of Mary."

"Hi Gina, how are you?"

"Oh I'm just fine. How are you?"

"Can't complain."

"Well, that's all we can ask for, right?"

"You got it! So how can I help you?"

"Well, my husband and I are moving into a condo. With the kids all grown and moved out, we really don't need that big house anymore."

"Sure, makes sense."

"Yes, and you know we have four nice couches, a pool table and a ping pong table, and I thought that you could probably use them for the Youth Center."

"Oh wow, that's really generous of you, but unfortunately, we can't really use them in the youth ministry center."

"Oh no, really?"

"Yeah...but you know, I could call a few families who might want some of it for their kids like in their basement or something like that."

"That would be great. I'd really appreciate that. I just don't want to throw them away."

"I hear ya. I'll let you know if you have any takers."

"Thanks a lot, Fred."

"No problem."

- *What are the social needs of the senior high youth in your parish?*

- *Couches, pool tables, ping pong tables and the like create a "hang out" atmosphere that inevitably is perceived by most to be a "club house" for a small group of "church kids": Agree or disagree?*

- *If permanent space is designated in your parish for youth ministry, how much of a voice should the youth have in deciding how it is furnished? How would you furnish it?*

- *If you were presented with plans for a new parish ministry building and were asked how to design the space designated for youth ministry (about the size of a basketball court), what would be your floor plan?*

PRIORITIES AND PARENTS

Here is a list of real-life excuses I have heard over the years:

"I can't go to Mass because I work every Saturday night and Sunday morning." —Eleventh grader whose father insists that she work on weekends

"I can't make night meetings because I have hockey practice." —Ninth grader who is referring to a year-round hockey club not affiliated with a school

"I really want to be on the retreat team, but we have games on Tuesdays, and when we play away, we have to stay until the JV game is over. Most times we don't get back until 8 PM. Then I have to have dinner and do my homework." —Twelfth-grade varsity field hockey player

"The post office doesn't always deliver all of our mail." —Mother who doesn't know the youth ministry schedule

"My daughter has to leave the retreat on Saturday morning because she has a *mandatory* soccer practice. I will bring her back for the closing Mass." —Father of a tenth grader who plays JV and sits on the bench for varsity

"I don't come to the retreat follow-up gatherings because they go until 9 PM, and I have to do my homework." —Tenth grader who goes to dance class twice a week until 10 PM

"My son will miss the Friday night portion of the retreat due to a family commitment. He will be there Saturday morning." —Father of a ninth grader whose "family commitment" was actually a Dave Matthews concert with his friends

"I couldn't come to the meeting because I didn't have a ride." —Eleventh grader whose parents went into the city for the day to see a play

"I have to leave the retreat for a few hours for basketball practice. If I miss the practice, the coach will bench me." —Twelfth grade retreat team co-director who goes to a Catholic high school

"I can't come...I have to leave early...I have to come late...because:

...SAT course...band practice...play practice... riding lessons...sweet sixteen party...school dance... mandatory school Mass...boy scouts...tennis tournament...mother's birthday...Saturday school... too much homework...parents won't let me...boss won't let me...coach won't let me...I have to babysit... I'm grounded...choir practice...college applications...

- *Based on your experience in youth ministry, how difficult/easy is it in your parish to schedule youth ministry events that are not in conflict with other extracurricular events?*

- *What kind of relationship does your parish have with the local schools and sports coaches?*

- *What is the downside of making youth ministry events mandatory?*

- *How would you deal with the situation of a young person who lies to you?*

- *How would you deal with a situation of a parent who lies to you?*

- *How can youth ministers, parents, schools, and coaches work together? At the very least, what might be some good steps to take toward working together?*

TO ADORE OR NOT TO ADORE

The time had come on the sophomore retreat for all to make their way to the church building for the next activity. Jerry, a senior on the retreat team, had prepared his witness talk on the topic of Eucharist. All gathered around the tabernacle as Jerry reverently opened the tabernacle door and exposed the Blessed Sacrament. He began to talk about Eucharist:

Do you see this? Some think that this is just a piece of bread. But this is not bread. This is Jesus! Earlier, when the priest consecrated this host, it ceased to be bread and became the Body of Christ. Imagine, Jesus himself right here in this room! Jesus is right here in this Blessed Sacrament and he wants us to adore him! He wants us feel his presence. Can you feel it? He is so holy, so great, and so awesome, and he is right here in the Blessed Sacrament.

Some do not believe that this is Jesus. Some think that it simply represents Jesus. But at the Last Supper, Jesus said "this is my Body," not this represents my Body. And so we believe Jesus when he says that this is his Body—right here in this Blessed Sacrament. And he gives it to us as a gift! In a moment, we are going to do something called Eucharistic Adoration. We are going to keep Jesus in the Eucharist right here, and we are going to each silently pray to him in our own way. I remember when I was a sophomore on this retreat, I prayed to the Eucharist so hard that I started to cry. That's what you have to do. You have to feel Jesus when you pray. Always remember, Eucharist is all about your personal relationship with Jesus, and this is our chance tonight to work on that relationship.

Jerry continued his talk on Eucharist by sharing stories with the group about all the mystical experiences he has had with the Blessed Sacrament and how he is thoroughly convinced that Jesus is truly present in the tabernacle. The group then engaged in a Eucharistic Adoration that seemed to go really well.

- *How do you feel about the practice of Eucharistic Adoration with adolescents?*

- *When I hear the word "Eucharist," I think of...*

- *If you worked with Jerry on his talk before the retreat, what sort of suggestions would you have made?*

- *What do you think are the factors in our Church and society that are leading to more and more young people having devotional eucharistic spiritualities like Jerry?*

CHOOSING PEER LEADERS

The new youth minister was looking forward to attending his first peer leader meeting. The group of peer leaders was put together by the previous youth minister, so the new guy was interested in seeing the kind of hand he had been dealt. There were eight peer leaders who showed up at the meeting: four sophomores, two juniors and two seniors. After introductions, the new youth minister asked everyone to share why they want to be a peer leader. They answered:

Sophomore 1: "I don't know. Maybe because it seems like a fun thing to do. I'm not really into sports or anything, so I guess I have some time to kill."

Sophomore 2: "Coming to youth group last year really helped me through some tough times. I don't get along with my parents very well, and being here at Church is a good break from all the arguing I do with them."

Sophomore 3: "Free food."

Sophomore 4: "Free food and free Dr. Pepper."

Junior 1: "I just really like coming here and hanging out. I can't stand all those conformist sheep at school who think they're so cool. It's not like that here. I like everyone here."

Junior 2: "Yeah, like at school, everybody is so concerned about what they wear and who's popular and where the party is being held on the weekend. This group isn't like that. I was in it last year and I can't even imagine not doing it again this year."

Senior 1: "To be completely honest, I don't really go to church. I just really like running Coffee Houses, and I can run them through this group. I put on two great Coffee Houses last year and want to do three this year. They're really fun, and we get a lot kids from around here and neighboring towns. At this point, I know how to run them in my sleep, so all you guys have to do is follow my lead."

Senior 2: "I'm a little different because I'm friends with (Senior 1) and she invited me here. I'm not even Catholic. I want to help out with the Coffee Houses, so here I am."

- *What would be your concerns if you were the new youth minister?*

- *What would be the next step in working with this team?*

- *What kind of requirements (if any) should there be for being a peer leader?*

- *How much of* Renewing the Vision *should we teach our peer leaders?*

- *What do you think about this book's suggestion of not having one peer leadership team for all of youth ministry (like in the above example), but rather having different leadership teams for each specific youth ministry event/program?*

HIRING OUTSIDE GROUPS

The diocesan newspaper does a write-up on a group of college students who have decided to carry over the leadership roles they played as high school age peer leaders within their parishes and schools into their college years. The article describes how the group is touring to different parishes in the area surrounding their college, running retreats and prayer nights and giving talks on various topics. They tout themselves as being completely coordinated by college students who love Christ and the Church and want to share their faith with their younger high school age peers. They liken their style to that of the LifeTeen movement. Of course, they are also musicians and incorporate upbeat Christian music into much of what they do and place great emphasis on Eucharistic Adoration. The article concludes by providing the information needed to contact the group in order to hire them for their services.

Predictably, someone like me writes a letter to the editor:

This letter is in response to last week's article on the youth program "staffed completely by college students." On the one hand, it is always inspiring and hopeful to see young adults wanting to share their faith with their younger peers. Too often in our Church, young adults do not exhibit any confidence in themselves as having authority (by right of their baptism) to pass on our faith and religious tradition. On the other hand, I am deeply concerned that this group seemingly does not have at least one pastorally experienced and educated adult collaborating with them and mentoring them.

When I first started as a coordinator of youth ministry in a parish, I had a great deal of experience as a teenager and young adult volunteer; however, my methods would have been very dangerous if I didn't have older and wiser colleagues mentoring me, especially in those early years when my operative theology was still very adolescent. By dangerous, I mean that my well-intentioned desire to share my faith in a creative way may not have always been pastorally sound.

Perhaps I would have been more concerned about creating fervor for Jesus among young people during a retreat than establishing a retreat process that stresses ongoing conversion and faith development. Perhaps I would have made primary the understanding of Eucharist as the Real Presence of Jesus in the Blessed Sacrament rather than stressing the understanding of Eucharist as the Real Presence of Jesus experienced through full, conscious, and active participation in liturgy and the mission work that follows.

I may never have acknowledged parents as the primary faith givers and sought to create opportunities for them to share their

faith with their teens. Perhaps I would have signed on with the ever-popular LifeTeen movement in order to see young people get enthusiastically involved, while paying no attention to its lack of long-term vision. I may have been content keeping the adolescent faith adolescent. I guess what I am saying is that as a professional youth minister and as an advocate for youth and their families, I would have serious reservations about bringing this group or any group that does not have an experienced and educated coordinator to my parish, nor would I invite any group that has a lack of long-term pastoral vision.

- *What points made in the letter do you agree with?*

- *What points do you disagree with?*

- *What has been your experience with hiring outside groups? How do the concerns in the letter to the editor apply to those experiences?*

- *How can outside groups be used by parishes in ways that foster ongoing faith formation?*

APPROPRIATE AND INAPPROPRIATE CONDUCT

The adult catechist working on the junior and senior retreat team seemed to have a really good rapport with a few of the upperclassers on the team who happen to be some of the more physically attractive young people of the group. She was always laughing with them at breaks and seemed to be sincerely interested in their lives. She developed a relationship with them to the point where they really felt at ease with her and were willing to share personal stuff with her. Soon it became common practice that the young people would either call the adult catechist on the phone or email her on a weekly basis to talk about their relationships with members of the opposite sex.

It became such a weekly ritual that the catechist soon was calling and emailing them just as much as they contacted her. The young people were not engaging in sexual intimacy or even thinking about it (at least the females were not), so the adult did not see herself as offering counsel, but rather thought of herself as an adult friend with whom the young people could talk about their relationships. Predictably, it didn't take long for one of the fathers of the young people to catch wind of all of this and call the youth minister asking, "Why is one of your catechists calling my son?"

- *What lines, if any, did the adult catechist cross?*
- *How difficult is it as a youth minister to not show "favorites"?*
- *If you were the youth minister in that parish, what would you say to the father?*
- *What similar "gray area" stories do you have from your youth ministry experience?*

NONESSENTIAL STRATEGIES?

The professor for the youth ministry certificate program begins the day's lesson.

Professor Now that we know all about youth ministry, we have to come up with a catchy name for it. Teenagers respond best to words that sound cool, but at the same time, we have to come up with a name that means something. We can't just call it "youth ministry" because that's too boring and doesn't attract teenagers. What we need is a good acronym. It need not only sound cool, but youthful. It needs to stand for something relevant to youth while at the same time convey a powerful message. So here's what we're going to do. I'm going to divide you up into four groups. I want you to brainstorm for a good acronym. Decide on the best one and be ready to present it to the class.

Twenty minutes go by...

All right, time's up. What do you have?

Group 1 We are calling our youth ministry: YUG!: Youth Under God. We thought that we would take the "under God" part of our pledge of allegiance and apply it here. Youth ministry is about young people living under God's commandments and watchful eye. Plus it sounds like something cool a caveman might say.

Professor Nice job! YUG is cool! Let's see how it works: "Hey, are you guys going to the YUG meeting tonight?" Excellent!

Group 2 We are calling our youth ministry: SOLID: Showing Our Love in Discipleship. SOLID is unbreakable, like Peter the rock. It is strong and unshakable. That's the kind of faith our young people will have if they get involved in SOLID youth ministry! "They will know we are Christians by our love!"

Professor "We went to the SOLID Mass last night. It was rockin'!" Yup, that works quite well. Nice job. Next?

Group 3 Okay, are you ready for this? YAWP: Youth Arising with Praise. Our group thought of that Walt Whitman quote: "I sound my barbaric yawp over the rooftops of the world." Youth ministry is about inspiring young people to rise up with Jesus and praise him. We shout it out: YAWP!

Professor Indeed you do! Your youth ministry is going to be a yawpin' good time! Derr...herr...herr!

Group 4 Well, we thought we'd keep it really simple and to the point: TAG!: Teens and God. Youth ministry is essentially about teens and God. Plus, we thought that the concept of the game of tag fits because what we do as Christians is try to catch others and tag them.

Professor   Tag, you're Christian! I like it. I like it a lot. Great job people. These are the kind of catchphrases that young people are attracted to. We have to be hip nowadays. We have to let our young people know that the Church isn't boring. How could something named "YUG" be boring? Acronyms like these are a good way to let young people know that we're with it and happening. We're cool!

- *What are the advantages and disadvantages of giving your parish youth ministry a name other than simply youth ministry (i.e. St. Andrew Youth Ministry)?*

- *From your experience, what would you guess are the percentages of youth in your parish who would be attracted by a catchy title because it sounds cool, youth who would be turned off by a catchy title because it seems too contrived, and youth who are indifferent?*

- *Whether you believe that the use of acronyms are helpful or not helpful, what other commonly used youth ministry strategies do you think are nonessential?*

HOW MANY SERVICE HOURS?

It is three weeks until confirmation and Bobby still needs to complete ten hours of required service in order to be confirmed. The truth be told, Bobby's heart is not really in it. He really does not care about being confirmed, but as an only child, he doesn't want to disappoint his parents, so he has done the minimum his parish requires of him. He has attended the required amount of confirmation classes and gone on the required retreat, but he just never got around to doing the service component. Now he is under the gun and

has to figure out how to get these ten hours in before it's too late.

The parish has a trip to the soup kitchen coming up, so his parents sign him up to help cook the meal at the parish center on a Saturday and also to go help serve it on a Sunday. His mom drops him off, and he silently follows the leader's instructions as he does his part. The group cooking consists of mainly the same crowd that cooks every month. They know what they're doing and have a good, efficient system of getting the work done quickly. It takes about an hour to complete. Bobby is picked up by his mom and dropped back off at the church the next morning. Once again, Bobby joins a group of parishioners who are "veterans" at soup kitchen runs. Bobby is very agreeable. He does whatever is asked of him, but it is obvious that he doesn't really want to be doing what he is doing. He is so focused on the tasks that are given to him that he is oblivious to his surroundings and what is really going on. He serves the food quietly and politely, looking up at the clock every few minutes or so, helps clean up, and listens to music on his headphones during the car ride home. Another three hours down. Only five hours left.

Two weeks until confirmation, and there are no scheduled service opportunities provided by the parish before the celebration. After a phone conversation with Bobby's parents, the youth minister decides to allow Bobby to finish his service requirement by coming in for an hour each day to help with office work. Bobby spends an hour each day folding and stuffing and sealing and stamping for all the parish mailings that week.

His service requirement is complete. Bobby is confirmed quietly and politely. He says to himself and eventually out loud to his friends, "Thank God that's over!"

- *Who fails Bobby in the previously described scenario? In what ways?*

- *What percentage of young people in your parish continue to participate in ongoing service opportunities after they are confirmed?*

- *What is your parish's policy regarding "service requirements"?*
- *How could Bobby's experience with the soup kitchen ministry have been more enriching?*

YOUTH MASS

Fr. Patrick, the parochial vicar, and Sr. Beatrice, the DRE, convince the pastor to add a Youth Mass to the weekend schedule at 6 PM on Sunday nights. This decision comes as a result of a couple of discussions at staff meetings about the issue of getting more teenagers to show up at Mass. The pastor isn't keen on the idea of having to say another Mass especially with a bunch of teenagers, so the younger Fr. Patrick suggests that he himself will preside at it each week. That's how strongly he feels about it. "If you want it, you got it!" says the pastor.

So the Youth Mass is born. The other thing that Fr. Patrick and Sr. Beatrice are happy about is that the Mass comes directly after the sixth, seventh, and eighth grade religious education and directly before the high school confirmation classes, so they make the Youth Mass part of the required curriculum.

Time goes by and Sr. Beatrice realizes that not all the kids are coming to Mass (only to religious ed). She and Fr. Patrick decide that not only is attendance to be taken at class, but at Mass as well. Before the young people take their seat in the pew, they must sign in with Sr. Beatrice standing in the back of church.

More time goes by and older parishioners start asking if they can come to the Youth Mass because it has a more convenient time than the regular parish Masses. So Fr. Patrick makes an announcement to the parish via letter and bulletin that all parishioners are invited to come to the Youth Mass. Some do.

After a year, Sr. Beatrice decides that each sharing group must prepare for the Liturgy of the Word three times per year. They are to work with their catechist at preparing the Prayers of the Faithful and taking on the lector and greeter ministries. Then a group of juniors and seniors who have started a Christian Rock band ask if they can play at the Youth Mass each week. Their wish is granted. Then Fr. Patrick trains four upperclassers to be Ministers of Communion at the Youth Mass. All is coming into place.

After two years, Sr. Beatrice and Fr. Patrick decide to take a survey among the youth about their impressions of the Youth Mass. Some express that they love it and look forward to it each week. Some say that even though it's better than "regular Mass," it's still boring. Most indicate that they are pretty much indifferent (The Youth Mass neither impresses them nor turns them off; it is what it is). Sr. Beatrice and Fr. Patrick view the results as very positive saying, "If a teenager says that they don't mind going to Mass, then we're ahead of the curve."

- *What are the advantages/disadvantages of the youth experiencing only Fr. Patrick as a leader of worship?*
- *What are the advantages/disadvantages of Sr. Beatrice taking attendance at Mass?*
- *What are the advantages/disadvantages of having a parish Mass that consists of mostly youth?*
- *What would you do differently if you were Sr. Beatrice and Fr. Patrick?*
- *"If a teenager says that they don't mind going to Mass, then we're ahead of the curve." Agree or disagree?*

FOR THE GLORY OF THE MESSAGE OR FOR THE MESSENGER?

Mike is given the opportunity to give the first witness talk on the junior and senior retreat entitled: *Being a Disciple.* Because he is impressed by his youth minister who often gives charismatic presentations, Mike decides that he is not going to write out his talk but just speak from the heart, presenting it with the same charismatic style. The youth minister encourages him to go for it.

The candidates are sitting on the floor. When he is introduced, he walks to the front of the room, grabs the microphone, paces back and forth in front of his designated seat and starts talking:

So you want to be a disciple. Or maybe you don't. I don't know. But I'm gonna tell you what it's all about. You may think it's about going to church and obeying all the rules, but really it's not about that. Being a disciple is all about having a personal relationship with Jesus Christ. You gotta let him in. Don't be the type of person who thinks he's too cool to be religious or to talk about Jesus. Because I can tell you right now, you are not too cool for Jesus. You gotta let Jesus in, let him shape your life. Jesus is there for you at all times. That's an amazing thing. Imagine, someone who is there for you 24/7. No matter what time of day or where you are, Jesus is there. Are you willing to acknowledge him? Are you willing to let him into your life? If you are not, what's holding you back? Maybe you don't really believe that Jesus is Lord of all. If you ask me: no way! There is no way that Jesus is not Lord. Once you let him into your life, you'll never doubt it. Like maybe you don't even think about how Jesus died for you. He died for *you*, man! He died on a cross for you. And you doubt him? Jesus sacrificed his life for you so that you can live! What have you done to pay him back? You gotta believe, man. Just believe in him and everything changes.

Mike continues his talk while investing a good amount of emotion into his body language. One half hour later, Mike finishes by performing a song that he wrote on his acoustic guitar entitled: *He Died for You.*

- *What reaction/concerns do you have regarding Mike and his witness talk?*

- *Was it right or wrong for the youth minister to encourage Mike to go for it?*

- *From your experience, how effective are charismatic presentations?*

- *How do you explain to young people the belief that Jesus died for us without going into a guilt trip?*

Dear Parent(s)/Guardian(s):

We would like to welcome you and your teen to senior high youth ministry. We are in the initiatory stages of developing a long and fruitful tradition of youth ministry in our parish, and we are looking forward to your participation in making that a reality.

We invite you to register your teen (registration enclosed). Each year, a new registration will be sent out to parents of high school age youth with the request that it be filled out and sent in with a donation.

All registered freshmen are automatically considered to be preparing for the sacrament of confirmation (unless otherwise informed). In our diocese, one participates in total youth ministry for at least one year at a high school level in order to come to understand what the life of a confirmed person entails. After sophomore year, the sacrament of confirmation is offered as a choice to all who come forward.

Confirmation preparation is a part of total youth ministry. That is why we are making no distinction between youth ministry and confirmation preparation. Likewise, we are making no distinction between post-confirmation and youth ministry. Participation in youth ministry is how juniors and seniors live out their confirmation within the parish community.

Please note the following:

1. Our calendar can be viewed on the youth ministry section of our parish web site: (your parish web site). If you are unable to view the web site, please let me know, and I will send you the paper copies.

2. Upon viewing the calendar, you will notice that there are certain events specifically geared toward freshmen, most notably: the Rite of Welcoming, the Freshman Retreat and Rite of Entrance, Freshman Follow-up Gatherings, and the Rite of Prayer.

3. At the Rite of Welcoming, we will have the opportunity to discuss the youth ministry process; if you would also like to meet with me individually, I would be happy to meet with you at your convenience.

Please know that we on the Ministerial Staff are *always* willing to listen to your concerns and to answer any questions at *any* time. Our phone number is (your phone number) or you can e-mail us at (your email address).

Thank you in advance for your support and trust, and we look forward to ministering with you.

Sincerely,
(your name)
Youth Minister

Notice: The first gathering of freshmen and their parents is the Rite of Welcoming at the 11:00 Mass on October 1 followed by lunch and Rite of Welcoming afternoon of reflection in the parish hall.

Dear (first name):

I would like to take this opportunity to do two things: 1. Introduce myself and 2. Welcome you to youth ministry. So, without further ado...

Hi, I am (your name). You should know who I am by now, but in case you don't, I'm your friendly neighborhood youth minister! I have been trained to do numerous things:

- Coordinate retreats for your enjoyment and enrichment
- Coordinate weekly gatherings where you can experience what it means to be a Catholic Christian
- Train and empower you to be leaders in the Church
- Provide you with service opportunities
- Involve you in prayer and worship within our parish in ways that will use your gifts and abilities.
- Speak on your behalf in those instances when society is not open to hearing the "youth voice"
- Always have an open door and a good listening ear should you have a problem that you would like to share with me

With that said, welcome to youth ministry! Check out the youth ministry sections of our parish web page: (your parish address).

Pretty soon, we will have our first gathering of the year, and we will be able to meet and greet you personally, as well as explain high school youth ministry in more detail.

Please call me (your phone number) or email me at (your email address) or stop by our office at any time if you have any questions or concerns.

I look forward to meeting you, and good luck with the beginning of HIGH SCHOOL!

Peace,
(your name)
Youth Minister

APPENDIX C
INITIAL INTERVIEW

Reminder: The goal of the initial interview is to create an environment of trust through "welcoming" conversation. There is no need to write all the answers down.

- Brothers/sisters and their ages:

- Personal interests:

- Hobbies:

- Favorite/least favorite subject in school:

- Favorite teacher of all time and why:

- Would you characterize yourself as an introvert or an extrovert? Explain.

- How do you feel about the parish in general (not the buildings)?

- What is the most memorable Mass you've ever been to?

- If there were one thing you would like to understand more clearly about God, Christianity, or Roman Catholicism, what would it be?

- In your own words and being completely honest, what does confirmation mean to you? (For those already confirmed substitute this question: In your own words and being completely honest, what does Catholicism mean to you?)

"Whoever welcomes this child in my name, welcomes me, and whoever welcomes me, also welcomes the one who sent me."

APPENDIX D
FINAL INTERVIEW GUIDELINES

Please have a twenty- to thirty-minute conversation, one on one, with your assigned candidates. Your conversation should incorporate the following questions:

- Do you wish to celebrate the sacrament of confirmation?

- If so, how has your participation in the parish helped you come to this decision?

- If not, what are the specific factors that have led you to this decision?

- Talk about your faith, how it has grown or formed, especially during the last two years.

- Talk about your service opportunities. How have they helped you understand what a confirmed person is supposed to be like?

- How do you plan to "live out your confirmation" through our parish? In other words, how are you going to continue your faith journey after the sacrament is celebrated?

Please inform (youth minister, pastor) of any individual that you feel needs follow-up before the sacrament is celebrated. Examples: someone whose sole reason for confirmation is, "Because my parents are making me"; someone who chooses not to be confirmed; someone who doesn't seem to understand the sacrament.

APPENDIX E
SMALL GROUP LEADERSHIP

1. YOUR ATTITUDE

Right The key to a good and meaningful small group is a trained small group leader who pays attention to details.

Wrong Training for small group leadership is a waste of time. Small groups should just answer the questions.

2. BODY LANGUAGE (S-O-L-D-E-R)

S (Square) You as the leader must be square to everyone in the small group. Of course, if you are sitting in a circle, this is impossible. "Square" is not to be taken literally. It means that your face can be seen by everyone in the group. Square also means that everyone is sitting at the same level.

O (Open) Never cross your arms. It gives the impression that you don't care about what someone is saying.

L (Lean) When someone is sharing of themselves in a small group, lean slightly toward that person.

D (Distance) You as the leader should always be at a fairly close distance to everyone in the group. You should never be under a table or covered in a blanket or lying down. Even though these things don't physically make you farther away, they do give the impression that your presence is far away.

E (Eye Contact) Whether you are speaking to someone or someone is speaking to the group, look that person in the eye.

R (Relax) Remembering to do S-O-L-D-E can make you stiff and awkward. That's why we throw an "R" at the end. In other words, do S-O-L-D-E in a Relaxed way.

3. SET-UP GROUP RULES

Everyone is expected to sit in a circle.

Everyone is expected to sit up (no lying down).

Everyone is expected to share and listen to others.

No one is to judge anyone else.

Confidentiality.

Respect for each other.

Give everyone permission to ask questions of one another. The more a small group becomes a conversation (rather than a question and answer session) the better.

4. BE PREPARED TO SHARE SOMETHING PERSONAL about each topic.

5. USE THE QUESTIONS AS A DISCUSSION STARTER, not a checklist. It is fine if your group spends the whole time on the first question.

6. REALLY LISTEN TO EACH PERSON. Avoid thinking about what you're going to say while someone else is speaking.

7. DO NOT GIVE ADVICE. Just listen and reassure each person that he/she is understood.

8. CALL SMALL GROUP MEMBERS BY NAME.

9. GET EVERYONE INVOLVED. Avoid developing a dependence on the "talkative person."

10. AVOID TANGENTS. If the group goes off on a tangent, nip it in the bud and get the group back on track.

11. LOOK FOR CONFUSED LOOKS, a raised eyebrow, a frown, etc., then follow up with a question for that person.

12. NEVER ASK "WHY" QUESTIONS.

13. SUMMARIZE! Say back in your own words previous comments that group members have made. This gives them a chance to clarify if you are not hearing them correctly and/or lets them know that you are really trying to connect with them.

14. CERTAIN PROBLEMS WARRANT THE BREAKING OF CONFIDENTIALITY. Drug and alcohol abuse, physical abuse, recent thoughts of suicide, running away, eating disorders, etc., are all valid reasons for breaking confidentiality. First, privately try to convince that person to talk to the youth minister. If you are unable to convince that person, then inform him/her that you have to tell an adult, and you are willing to do that with or without his/her blessing.

15. RECOGNIZE THAT YOU ARE NOT A TRAINED COUNSELOR and that you will do more harm than good if you try to counsel someone with a serious problem.

16. SPEND TIME OUTSIDE YOUR SMALL GROUP with each member of your small group—during free time, meals, large group, etc.

APPENDIX F
WHAT TO AVOID WHEN
WRITING A WITNESS TALK

PREACHING Whenever you find yourself using "you should..." or "you have to..." statements, chances are that your talk is getting too preachy. Ninety percent of your talk should be about you—your story, your thoughts, and your feelings.

TEACHING The talk outlines given to you are full of information. However, this information is not meant for you to regurgitate in your talk. It is there for your own background only. You are not expected or asked to teach others about some aspect of Scripture or tradition.

SPEECHING A witness talk is not simply public speaking. You certainly will want to utilize basic public speaking structures (i.e., introduction, body, conclusion), but it need not be too regimented and objective. Metaphor is the language of our God, so feel free to break the confines of a typical speech and delve more into your creative side.

DEPRESSING STORIES THAT OFFER NO HOPE For whatever reason, sometimes peer-led retreats tend to be one sob story after another. It can even get to the point where each team leader tries to "out-sob" each other. It is fine to talk about difficult times in your life in your witness talk as long as it relates to your topic and as long as the hope of our faith shines through.

OVERLY DRAMATIC/CHARISMATIC This has more to do with your presentation, which we will cover later, but does relate to how your talk is written. Each witness talk glorifies some message of the gospel. Be mindful of this as you write your talk. Constantly ask yourself, "Am I glorifying the message or the messenger?" Overly dramatic and/or charismatic presentations tend to glorify the messenger over the message.

1 If you feel like you are going slow enough, you're not! You must go so slow that it pains you.

2 If you feel like you are loud enough, you're not! You must be so loud that it pains you.

3 Look up during the last three to four words of every sentence and sustain that look until you finish the sentence. Don't worry if you lose your place since there is a natural pause at the end of every sentence anyway.

4 Use a bible or lectionary when proclaiming Scripture with a more uptight posture and holding the book high and to the side.

5 Lean forward and sit on the edge of your seat unless you are wearing a skirt, in which case you should sit up straight.

6 Use inflection in your voice, especially when you are quoting someone.

7 Your talk should sound as if you are speaking to us, not reading to us. Someone who has reached the level of "Magna Cum Laude Talk Delivery" would not even have a talk to read, but rather note cards or an outline from which to speak.

8 Be aware of your hands and feet, and any other body part that may be a distraction to the hearer.

9 Remember all the time and effort you put into your talk and what a waste it would be if people could not connect with you because you did not follow rules 1 though 8.

10 Relax!

7:00 PM Welcome and Community Building

- Divide everyone into three groups

- Everyone sits in circle based on how they rate the week past (1-10)

- What number did you choose, why?

7:15 PM Gathering Prayer: Large Group

- Light Advent candles

- Prayer leader speaks of Mary's example of "straight living," never straying off the path between her and God, before inviting all to pray the Hail Mary

7:20 PM Change of Heart Exercise

7:45 PM Witness Talk entitled: "Straightening the Curves" given by one of the team leaders

8:00 PM Small Group Discussion: Divide everyone up into groups of eight. Each group should have at least one team leader and one adult catechist.

8:20 PM Large Group Catechesis

8:30 PM Singing/Snack break

9:00 PM Candle Signing Ritual and Closing Prayer

CHANGE OF HEART EXERCISE

1. Divide everyone into groups of three. Try to have one team leader in each group.

2. Give everyone the following list of virtues:

- *Prudence:* (Cardinal Virtue) Prudence is the virtue that helps us discern, in every circumstance, our true good and to choose the right means of achieving it. The prudent person figures out the right thing do.

- *Justice:* (Cardinal Virtue) Justice consists in the firm and constant will to give God and neighbor their due. The just person is fair and gives everyone their rights.

- *Fortitude:* (Cardinal Virtue) Fortitude ensures firmness (strength) in difficulties and constancy in the pursuit of good. The strong person overcomes fear, especially when courage is needed to do the right thing.

- *Temperance:* (Cardinal Virtue) Temperance moderates the attraction of the pleasures of the senses and provides balance in the use of created goods. The temperate person is not controlled by impulsive desires, but uses reason based on what is honorable.

- *Faith:* (Theological Virtue) By faith, we believe in God and all that God has revealed to us and that the Church proposes for our belief. It is believing that God is real and present to us and is experienced all the time.

- *Hope:* (Theological Virtue) By hope we desire, and with steadfast trust await from God, eternal life and the graces to merit it. Hope is the ability to not give up on yourself and/

or on others because God does not give up on us.

- *Charity:* (Theological Virtue) By charity, we love God above all things and our neighbor as ourselves for love of God. Charity is loving God through loving others and loving others through loving God. It is giving yourself away like a gift to others.

(Based on the *Catechism of the Catholic Church* #1835-1844)

3. Each individual is asked to look over the virtues and rate each from 1 to 10. Example: Prudence. A "10" for prudence would mean that I judge myself to be exceptionally prudent. A "1" would mean that I judge myself to be extremely non-prudent.

4. Give each group a piece to a puzzle and ask groups to write on both sides in bold letters the one virtue that the whole group scored the lowest on.

5. Ask one member from each group to paste their piece of the puzzle onto the board.

6. The puzzle forms a heart. (outline the pieces of the puzzle beforehand on the board so that everyone knows where to paste the pieces.)

7. Explain the following before introducing the witness talk:

Mathematics teaches us that the quickest and most direct way to get from one point to another is a straight line. Both John the Baptist and the prophet Isaiah (quoted in today's gospel), must have understood this well. When it is proclaimed, "Prepare the way of the Lord, make straight his paths," we are being called to continually transform our lives in such a way that we remove all obstacles between us and God. We are reminded that when we sin, we

create barriers or roadblocks or mountains or valleys or unnecessary windings between us and God. The more sin we are able to recognize and remove from our day-to-day lives, the straighter our paths will be.

John the Baptist proclaims "Repent, for the kingdom of heaven is at hand!" The Greek word for this is *metanoia*, meaning "change your heart." During the season of Advent, we slow down (or least we're supposed to slow down) and reflect on our path to God. We discern what we need to change within ourselves in order to have a more direct path stretched out between us and God.

WITNESS TALK: STRAIGHTENING THE CURVES

Purpose To reflect on the Second Sunday of Advent (Year A), in particular the readings from the previous Sunday, and connect its message of "making a straight path" to your everyday life.

Movie Clip Show the clip at the end of *The Grinch Who Stole Christmas* where the Grinch has a change of heart on top of the mountain and decides to give all the toys back.

Outline of your Talk

- Introduction/Proclaim Matthew 3:1–12
- Connect the gospel to the theme of your talk
- Show the movie clip and explain how it relates to the gospel
- Personal story: Describe a time when you acted like a Grinch and had a "change of heart." In other words, how were you going astray, and what did you do in order to straighten out your path?
- Talk about being in high school and how it's easy to not be like Jesus. What are all the

things that are obstacles between you and Jesus? How does clearing a straight path to love in your heart make life better? Give an example from your life.

- Conclusion

SMALL GROUP DISCUSSION

- What struck you about the talk?

- Name some obstacles in your life that prevent you from preparing a straight path between you and the Lord.

- What can you do about these obstacles?

- What will you do about these obstacles?

LARGE GROUP CATECHESIS

1. One representative from each group shares with everyone a summary of how their group's discussion went.

2. The group leader connects the gospel theme to Catholic teaching:

We, the people of God begin the Church year with Advent and the focus on *metanoia* as a way to remember our people's "long preparation for the Savior's first coming," but more importantly as a way to "renew our ardent desire for his second coming" (*Catechism of the Catholic Church* #524). In other words, we begin the Church year by preparing ourselves for the end of the world. The deep and quiet color of violet or purple used during this season reminds us of the pre-dawn sky. We know through faith and hope that light is coming, but for now we must wait in joyful anticipation and quiet preparation.

So how do we prepare? How do we, like the Grinch, change our hearts? How do we make a straight path? The Church teaches that the most direct way to God is the way of Jesus. It is a way of virtuous living. To

be virtuous is to be more than practicing something for its own sake; it means "being" the presence of Jesus in the world. The practice of the virtues helps us do this.

"What would Jesus do?" is a good question to ask, but I think that Jesus himself would say that it is not good enough. It's better to ask: How would Jesus "be" toward others? That is the question of a true disciple.

CANDLE SIGNING RITUAL AND CLOSING PRAYER

1. Get everyone into one big circle. Have everyone recall the "virtue heart puzzle" that we put together at the beginning of this gathering. In it we placed the virtues that we need to work on in order to change our hearts and make a straight path to God.

2. Explain that for the closing prayer, we are going to ask everyone to pass the first two Advent candles around in opposite directions. When the candle comes to you, share with the group in detail or in just a sentence which virtue(s) you would like to work on this Advent season. It could be the one you chose earlier or it could be any other characteristic of Jesus that you want to have for yourself.

3. Once you have shared out loud, write the virtue on the candle with the sharpie (not too big).

4. When finished, we will place the candles in the middle with the other two Advent candles, light them and conclude with a shared prayer.

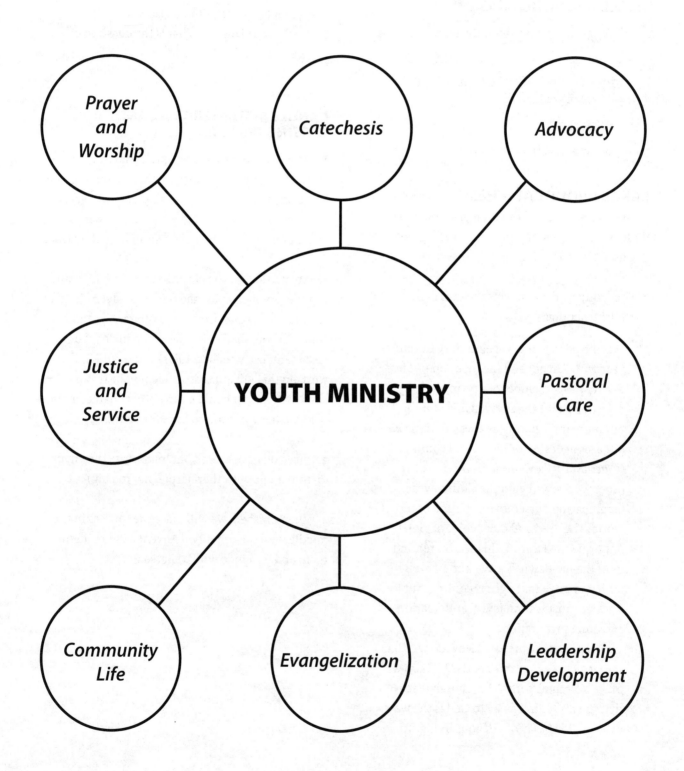

Prayer and Worship

Catechesis

Advocacy

Justice and Service

YOUTH MINISTRY

Pastoral Care

Community Life

Evangelization

Leadership Development

APPENDIX J
FOUR YEARS OF YOUTH MINISTRY

EXAMPLE ONE: MUSICAL MIKE	EXAMPLE TWO: DANCING DEBRA	EXAMPLE THREE: SOCCER SAM	EXAMPLE FOUR: MARCHING BAND MARTHA
9th Grade	**9th Grade**	**9th Grade**	**9th Grade**
Rite of Welcoming, Fall Retreat, A Few Follow-ups, Living Stations, Make Sandwiches, Rite of Prayer, Choir/Band, Weekly Mass	*Winter Retreat, Food Pantry, Catholic Youth Rally, Parish Festival, Rite of Welcoming, Rite of Prayer, Weekly Mass*	*Rite of Welcoming, Spring Retreat, Rite of Prayer*	*Nothing*
10th Grade	**10th Grade**	**10th Grade**	**10th Grade**
Choir/Band, Fall Retreat, Follow-ups, Rite of Creed, Soup Kitchen, Rite of Covenant, Rite of Confirmation, Weekly Mass	*Winter Retreat, Follow-ups, Soup Kitchen, Weekly Mass, Sell Christmas Wreaths, Rite of Creed, Rite of Covenant, Rite of Confirmation*	*Food Pantry, Spring Retreat, Two Follow-ups, Rite of Creed, Mission Week*	*Fall Retreat, Follow-ups, Soup Kitchen, Choir/Band, Catholic Youth Rally*
11th Grade	**11th Grade**	**11th Grade**	**11th Grade**
Freshman Retreat Team, Feed the Homeless, Appalachia Fundraisers, Junior/Senior Retreat, Follow-ups, Mission Trip, Weekly Mass, Choir/Band	*Pastoral Advisory Council, Minister of Communion, NCYC, Weekly Mass*	*Mission Fundraisers, Rite of Covenant, Rite of Confirmation, Lector, Mission Week, Weekly Mass*	*Rite of Welcoming, Rite of Prayer, Junior/Senior Retreat, Rite of Creed, NCYC, Nursing Home, Rite of Covenant, Rite of Confirmation, Choir/Band*
12th Grade	**12th Grade**	**12th Grade**	**12th Grade**
Feed the Homeless, Junior/Senior Retreat Team, Coffee House, Weekly Mass, Choir/Band	*Pastoral Advisory Council, Minister of Communion, Weekly Mass, World Youth Day*	*Mission Fundraisers, Mission Week, Lector, Weekly Mass*	*Retreat Team, Parish Festival, Choir/Band, Living Stations, Junior/Senior Retreat, Follow-ups*

4. PERIOD OF FORMATION CONTINUED

Get Serious Stage

Prayer and Worship	Community Life	Catechesis and Pastoral Care	Justice and Service and Advocacy	Leadership Development and Evangelization
Youth Choir, Weekly Mass, Lector Training, Rite of Creed	*Parish Events, Diocesan Events*	*Sophomore Retreat, Sophomore Follow-up Gatherings, Rite of Covenant Evening of Reflection*	*Feed the Homeless, Food Pantry, Nursing Home, Soup Kitchen, Mission Help Weeks*	*Freshman Retreat Team, World Youth Day, National Catholic Youth Conference*

The time has come for you to start thinking about choosing a confirmation name and sponsor.

First, we ask you to choose a confirmation name for yourself. Your first name is your "Christian name" or "baptismal name" and indicates your membership in the Christian community. Confirmation completes baptism; therefore it is strongly urged that you take your baptismal name (as long as it is the name of a saint). If you choose a new name, it is to be a saint's name. Every saint is known for particular qualities and virtues. On the other side of this sheet, you are asked to explain why you chose your name, and by imitating the qualities of this saint, how you can become a better Christian. We recommend that you find information about your saint.

Second, you are asked to choose a confirmation sponsor. You do not journey alone within the Christian community. Along the way, you make ties with certain members who demonstrate in their lives what it means to be a Catholic. A sponsor at confirmation is someone who stands up for you before the community, presents you to the bishop, and witnesses the anointing with the chrism. Your sponsor should serve as someone you can turn to for help and guidance as you continue your journey of faith in the years ahead. Your Sponsor must be a practicing confirmed Catholic who will be eighteen years of age or older by (date of confirmation Mass) and is not your parent. If your sponsor is not a member of (your parish), please indicate the parish in which he/she is registered on the back of this sheet. If it makes sense to you in your life, we recommend that you choose one of your godparents for your sponsor.

Please return this sheet to the parish office by _____

Full Name (*as you would like it to appear on your confirmation certificate*):

_____

Address: _____

What name have you chosen for yourself as your confirmation name?

_____

By imitating the qualities of the saint whose name you share, how can you become a better Christian? (*Don't know much about your Saint? Go to* www.newadvent.org.)

_____

_____

_____

Who have you chosen to be your sponsor? _____

What is your relationship to this person? _____

Why have you chosen this person to be your sponsor?

_____

_____

_____

In what parish is your sponsor registered? _____

If you were baptized at the parish, what was the date? _____

(*If you were not baptized at the parish, please include a copy of your baptismal certificate when returning this sheet.*)

At this moment in my life, I choose to be a Catholic Christian because God has been revealed to me in many ways...through a boy who helped me realize my self-worth, through an acquaintance who offered her guidance after I desperately prayed for it, through a mother and father whose love knows no limits. God has been revealed to me through the ocean, one of the most awesome parts of creation. God has led me on a searching journey and has shown me that friendship and love are more important than image and that fulfillment flourishes from love. I love Catholicism because Catholics believe that developing a communal relationship with Jesus Christ is as important as developing an individual relationship with him. As Catholics, we do not aim to control people; rather, through our actions we aim to reveal the Holy Spirit and thus transform the world. We are a community of believers, and we believe that God loves all of creation just the same.

PURPOSE To explore what being Catholic means to you at this stage in your life and your faith development. To give witness to others that practicing your Catholic religion helps you live out your Christian mission.

1. FAITH AND RELIGION

- **Faith:** your belief in God (whatever that perception may be)
- **Religion:** how you express your faith
- Christianity is your tradition. Define Christianity in your own words.
- Catholicism is your religion. Define Catholicism in your own words.

2. STAGES OF FAITH

- **Experienced Faith:** having a specific faith solely because that's what you were taught as a child. Typical for little children. Describe yourself when your faith was in this category. Do you know anyone who is still in this stage of faith?

- **Affiliative Faith:** faith that is beyond solely what was taught to you, yet is unquestioned and accepted blindly. You don't really understand your faith, you just accept it. Typical of later childhood. Describe yourself when your faith was in this category. Do you know anyone who is still in this stage of faith?

- **Searching Faith:** no longer just accepting your faith. Questioning your faith and the people who are passing it on to you. To some, it seems as if there is little or no faith. "Why should I go to Mass if I don't get anything out of it? Why should I believe what other people say about God?" These are the questions of a person with a searching faith, typical of most teenagers and some adults. Describe yourself when your faith was in this category. Do you know anyone who is still in this stage of faith?

- **Owned Faith:** you understand the beliefs of faith and personally choose to belong to that faith tradition. Typical of young adults and up.
  1. In what ways do you own your Christian faith?
  2. In what ways do you own your Catholic religion?
  3. In what ways do you not own your Christian faith?
  4. In what ways do you not own your Catholic religion?

3. PRACTICING CATHOLICISM IS LIVING OUT THE MISSION OF JESUS

- Read Luke 4:16–21: Jesus proclaims what his mission is, and in doing so, gives us our mission.

- As an active member of your parish, answer the following:
  1. How is the Spirit of Jesus alive and well in me?
  2. How do I bring good news to the poor (show the unloved love)?
  3. How do I proclaim liberty to captives? Who are the captives in my parish community and how do I help them?
  4. How do I bring sight to the blind (help others see the value of loving others)?
  5. How do I set free the oppressed (work toward social justice)?
  6. How do I announce that the time has come when the Lord will save his people (how do people meet Jesus when they meet me)?

4. CONCLUSION: SUM UP THE POINT YOU ARE MAKING

REFERENCES

Aubrey, A. "Le Projet Pastoral du Rituel de l'Initiation des Adultes." *Ephemerides Liturgicae* (Vol. 88, No. 3), 1974, pp. 180-82.

Bausch, William J. *A New Look at the Sacraments.* Mystic, CT: Twenty-Third Publications, 1983.

Catechism of the Catholic Church. New York: Bantam Doubleday Dell Publishing Group, 1994.

Center for Applied Research in the Apostolate. *Special Report: Young Adult Catholics.* Washington, DC: Georgetown University, 2002.

Congregation for the Clergy. *General Directory for Catechesis.* Washington, DC: United States Catholic Conference, 1997.

Congregation for Divine Worship. *The Rites of the Catholic Church, Volume 1.* New York: Pueblo Publishing Company, 1969.

Duggan, R.D. "Lectionary-Based Catechesis: Conflicting Views." *Church Magazine,* Spring 1992, pp. 18-20.

———. "Parish as a Center for Forming a Spiritual People," *New Theology Review* (Vol. 11, No. 4), 1998, pp. 15-26.

Erikson, E.H. *Childhood and Society* (Second Edition). New York: W.W. Norton, 1963.

Fowler, J. *Stages of Faith: The Psychology of Human Development and the Quest for Meaning.* San Francisco: Harper Collins, 1995.

Harris, M. *Fashion Me a People: Curriculum in the Church.* Louisville: Westminster/John Knox Press, 1989.

Himes, M.J. *Doing the Truth in Love.* Mahwah, NJ: Paulist Press, 1995.

Huebsch, Bill. *Handbook for Success in Whole Community Catechesis.* Mystic, CT: Twenty-Third Publications, 2004.

Ivory, T.P. "The Restoration of the Catechumenate as a Norm for Catechesis." *The Living Light* (Vol. 13, No. 1) Summer 1976, pp. 225-35.

Mandry, J. and M. *The New Antioch Manual: For a Parish-Based Youth Ministry.* Dubuque: Wm. C. Brown Company, 1986.

Milner, A.P. *The Theology of Confirmation.* Notre Dame: Fides Publishers, 1971.

National Conference of Catholic Bishops. *Communities of Salt and Light: Reflections on the Social Mission of the Parish.* Washington, DC: United States Catholic Conference, 1994.

———. *Sharing the Light of Faith: National Catechetical Directory for Catholics of the United States.* Washington, DC: United States Catholic Conference, 1979.

National Federation for Catholic Youth Ministry. *The Challenge of Adolescent Catechesis: Maturing in Faith.* Washington, DC: National Federation for Catholic Youth Ministry, Inc., 1986.

Rahner, K. *A New Baptism in the Spirit: Confirmation Today.* Denville, NJ: Dimension Books, 1975.

Roberto, John. *Generations of Faith.* Naugatuck: Center For Ministry Development, 1995.

Shea, J.J. "The Superego God." *Pastoral Psychology* (Vol. 43, No. 5), 1995, pp. 333-51.

———. *Finding Faith Again.* Lanham, MD: Rowman and Littlefield Publishers, Inc., 2005.

Smith, C. and M. Lundquist Denton. *Soul Searching: The Religious and Spiritual Lives of American Teenagers.* New York: Oxford University Press, 2006.

Songy, James B. *Questions and Answers for Catholics.* Mystic, CT: Twenty-Third Publications, 2000.

U.S. Bishops. *Empowered by the Spirit: Campus Ministry Faces the Future.* Washington, DC: United States Catholic Youth Conference, Inc., 1986.

U.S. Bishops. *Renewing the Vision: A Framework for Catholic Youth Ministry.* Washington, DC: United States Catholic Youth Conference, Inc., 1997.

Zanzig, T. *Confirmed in a Faithful Community: Coordinator's Manual.* Winona: Saint Mary's Press, 1995.